City Lives

City Lives

True stories of changed lives from the workplace

Marcus Nodder

10 Publishing
a division of 10ofthose.com

Copyright © 2018 by Marcus Nodder

First published in Great Britain in 2018

(Reprinted once)

British Library Cataloguing in Publication Data
A record for this book is available from the British Library

ISBN: 978-1-912373-09-3

Designed and typeset by Pete Barnsley (CreativeHoot.com)

Printed in Denmark by Nørhaven

10Publishing, a division of 10ofthose.com
Unit C, Tomlinson Road, Leyland, PR25 2DY, England

Email: info@10ofthose.com
Website: www.10ofthose.com

To my family with love – Lina,
Sebastian, Reuben, Harriet, Nelson.

I would like to thank the St Peter's Barge church family and staff for their generosity in giving me study leave to write this book – and for their ongoing love and partnership. Thank you to the people who are the subject of this book for making time to be interviewed and allowing their stories to be told. And thank you to the team at 10ofthose, especially to Julie Hatherall for her work as editor.

Contents

Introduction

A Serbian friend of mine grew up in Belgrade in a culture in which atheism is the norm. He moved to the UK and is now earning his living as a successful banker. He's not a Christian, but in recent years has found himself asking questions about life, the universe, and everything. When I mentioned the idea of this book to him he wrote back, 'It's perfect for people like me. To me there's something mystical about how one becomes a Christian and I think your book will make it more accessible for many. It will encourage people to try to find God, or continue to explore and not give up if they have started the journey already.' The book tells the true stories of fourteen people who are followers of Jesus Christ and living that out in their city lives. Some were brought up as Christians, but most of them weren't. For some coming to Christian faith was a gradual process of investigation; for others a dramatic experience.

My friend added, 'I think particularly valuable would be stories from people who became Christian without having a major life crisis or difficulty, as in those circumstances some could dismiss their faith as escapism.' The stories in this book actually cover both categories, because for some it does take a crisis to wake them up to their need of God. But the concern about escapism is understandable. And so the question about whether Christian faith is just a psychological crutch is one the book addresses, along with others that are listed on the contents page.

Not only do the ways these people came to faith in Christ vary widely, but also the spheres in which they have gone on to live out their faith in Christ cover quite a spectrum – from the Premier League to Parliament, from fashion to finance, from music to the military, from baking to business, from singing to sport. Though very different, the people whose stories are told here do have at least two things in common.

Firstly, and most importantly, they are living all-in for Jesus Christ. All of us have a centre circle in life. What goes in that centre circle is what drives us. It's what gets us out of bed in the morning. It's what we are living for. It varies from person to person, but we all have something, or someone, in there. A true Christian is someone who is living for Jesus Christ, the one who died on the cross as their rescuer and was raised to life as their ruler. He is in the centre circle. Let me illustrate this with a question: in an egg and bacon breakfast, what is the difference between the chicken and the pig? The answer: the chicken is involved, but the pig is committed. That is the true Christian – not just involved but committed to Jesus. And that is what this book is about – how people came to such all-in faith in Christ, and what that looks like in everyday life.

Secondly, these men and women are 'high-flyers' who have risen to positions of prominence. Given this focus on Christian faith in the fast lane, a couple of qualifications are needed to avoid misunderstanding. The first one is that this is not saying people at the top of the food chain are worth more than others in God's sight. God's value system is not ours. But from a human interest perspective it's fun for those of us on the lower slopes to see what the view is like from the summit. It should also challenge the notion that Christian faith is only for the unintelligent, gullible, or weak. The second qualification is that this is not saying if you become a Christian you will become successful or wealthy. The Bible doesn't promise that. Countless followers of Christ around the world are at the bottom of the food chain.

Eighteen months ago my Serbian friend and I started meeting up once a week to read a bit of the Bible and discuss it together. Since then we've worked our way through John's Gospel, as well as other parts of the Bible. At the time of writing he's not become a Christian, but wants to keep exploring. If you're anything like him, this book is for you.

1

Paralympic Medallist
Stef Reid

Why does God allow suffering?

It was 15 years ago, but Stef remembers everything as if it were yesterday. She had been staying with friends at a cottage on a lake in Canada for a long weekend. They woke up on the final morning to perfect conditions for tubing on mirror-like water behind her friend's motor boat. She was on one of the two tubes being pulled along at adrenalin-pumping speed, having the time of her life, with the driver doing his best to flip them off. After coming off, she was treading water, daydreaming and enjoying the view, waiting for the boat to come round and pick her up. As it turned to head in her direction and got closer, she realised it was going too fast and hadn't seen her.

Being a strong swimmer she made the split-second decision to dive down, hold her breath and wait for the boat to pass over her. She didn't get far. She had forgotten she had a life jacket on. Everything went dark. When she surfaced she was in shock, but thought she was okay. She says, 'My friends on the boat were yelling and screaming and freaking out, but I thought I'd been lucky. I then noticed that all around me the water was red. I didn't feel right but didn't know why. I was confused. My back was itchy. I reached down and my hand went inside.' The propeller had caught her across her back and split her right foot from top to bottom.

It was a bank holiday Monday, and they were in the middle of nowhere. An ambulance rushed her to the local doctor's surgery. They managed to contact her parents, but when they came in to see Stef she realised they had come to say goodbye. She remembers feeling angry and thinking, 'You're giving up. I'm not done yet.' After that her memory fades as the painkillers took over. She made it to the hospital and the best surgeon in Canada was flown in. Amazingly she survived. That day she did not lose her life, though she did lose her right foot. But Stef remarks that she gained something worth even more. It was as result of the accident that she came to faith in Christ, and through him to a new life of knowing God and living for him.

Stef was born in New Zealand to British parents. They weren't Christian but respected Christian values, so when they moved to Canada they were more than happy to send their daughter to a Christian school in Toronto. Through this education she observes, 'I grew up with a very good factual knowledge about the Bible, but it was not translated into my heart at all. I knew a lot, but didn't love God or care what his will was for my life.' Twelve months before the accident, at the end of one class, she recalls saying in her head, 'God, my heart is not in this. If you want me, you'll need to make this real for me.' A year later he did just that.

As Stef lay in the ambulance, she remembers feeling very tired and just wanting to sleep. A paramedic was saying to her, 'Stef, you must stay awake. If you go to sleep, we might not be able to wake you up.' She knew that death was at hand, and all of a sudden she was very scared. She says,

> A wave of terror came over me. I knew that if I died then, I wouldn't go to heaven. And it was terrifying. I knew in my heart that I hadn't lived for God but selfishly for my own will. And I now saw how wrong that was. I was sorry and desperate for a second chance. So I prayed my first honest prayer to God and begged him to save my life.

And he did. So began a spiritual journey that would lead three years later to her publicly professing faith in Christ in baptism.

The spiritual change Stef came to experience was so profound that she describes becoming 'a completely different person'. And the change was so good that she even comments,

> I would love to have my foot back, but I would not exchange it for the person I have become as a result of losing it. It's a

7

gift in your mid-teens to learn what really matters in life. I'm very grateful for that ...

At 15 no-one really contemplates their death or thinks they're going to die at some point. But facing death I could see what matters and what doesn't. Everything I had been living for had been with the wrong intention. It had all just been about me wanting to be successful. But my accident completely changed how I valued things. Lots of things seem quite shallow against the backdrop of death.

For example, Stef came to see that spending two hours getting ready for a party didn't matter, but people did:

What mattered now was relationships with people. That took on a new meaning for me. When I went back to school I was worried that no-one would like me because I had nothing to offer. Before I'd played sport for two hours after school while waiting for my mum to pick me up. Now I had two hours to do nothing. But it meant I could spend time talking to people, and I realised there is so much value in that connection. I began thinking about people differently and what makes people worthwhile. I wanted to start seeing people the way God sees them.

Everything in her life changed. Stef became more concerned with the quality of her heart and mind, and protecting that. She would ask herself questions about how her time was being spent and how her life was oriented.

Her goal was to act in-line with God and his values. She says, 'I now saw that God had given me time and energy and abilities, and the question was how I could use them to please him rather than for me.' But these changes were far from immediate. It all took time, and things were not instantly fine.

When her mum walked into the recovery room she told her, 'Stef, I'm so sorry. The doctors did everything they could, but they had to amputate.' Stef remembers the moment clearly: 'I was devastated. I was so thankful to be alive, but I wasn't sure I wanted to experience life as an amputee and give up on my dream to be a professional athlete. I didn't want to look different to everyone else.' For the first week she felt angry and bitter, and was horrible to family and friends. But day seven was a turning point. Nurse Claudette walked in and told her it was time to eat and to be helped to bathe. Stef refused, having stopped caring about anything. At that point the nurse confronted her, firmly but lovingly, saying, 'That is enough. You need to smile. There is a 12-year-old girl in the ward below you who's lost both her feet!'

Stef was a bit taken aback at being challenged so directly, but the nurse had read her exactly right. She knew Stef was unbelievably competitive and that she wouldn't be able to bear the thought that someone younger might be coping better. Stef explains, 'It set off a spark of life in me again. She reminded me of who I was. I realised that I may have lost my foot, but I hadn't lost who I am; that I was still the same person. I realised that life carries on and could still be a great life full of joy and happiness.'

The anger Stef had initially felt was partly directed towards God. She says that she never felt any anger towards the driver of the boat. It was just an accident. He was a good guy, her best friend's older brother, and she actually felt sorry for him and the psychological trauma he had to deal with as a result. She went to visit him later and reassured him: 'I'm really happy. You haven't ruined my life.' But with God it was different. Unlike the driver, God not only knew this would happen, but surely could have stopped it. This raises a difficult question for the Christian: 'Why would God allow this?' It was a question Stef asked straight away: 'Waking up in the recovery room I was very thankful that God had saved my life, but then, finding my leg had been amputated, I was angry. Why would God take away the one thing I loved most?'

She had loved sport all her life, from age two or three onwards. It had always been part of her existence. She had loved challenging her body and running fast. She had been into ballet, basketball, cross-country running, and swimming. Then it had been rugby. Her talent and passion had been spotted early, and her dream to play at international level looked like it might become reality. And then this had occurred. It seemed so cruel. If God really is good and loving, and if he is in control, why would he allow this to happen?

But as she lay in the recovery room, she says, 'Although angry and frustrated, I was also at peace and could feel the presence of God. I was in a strange place – angry with God and yet at the same time at peace with him. I had to decide if I would trust God,' She decided she would:

I made the decision, leaving my hospital bed, that I would give the Creator of the world the benefit of the doubt! I would allow him to work in my life as he saw fit. He didn't let me down. There would be periods of mourning and deep sadness, but God was there with me. Actually there was so much grace and joy in the process – and more joy in my life after the accident than before. The way I valued and saw things totally changed.

I had been so scared to die that amputation was not so bad against that backdrop. Three months later I was fitted with my first walking leg.

She remembers her first time back at school with her artificial leg. She tried to sneak in at the side of the room during assembly, but people saw her and everyone started clapping and cheering. She says, 'It was a beautiful moment that made so many people happy.'

But the 'Why?' question is one she had to work through. Although there are no simple answers, there are a number of perspectives Stef has found helpful as a Christian. Firstly, even when she was in hospital feeling bitter, she was also aware that it was a bit rich her turning on God because of this one bad thing that had happened, when over the previous 15 years she hadn't once thanked God for anything. Secondly, she came to realise that 'God is more concerned with my growth than my comfort'. She explains, 'I don't want to stay as I am. I want to grow in maturity and in my faith. I want a God who will challenge me. This was the most loving thing for my long-term growth. The biggest growth periods in life come when we have the biggest obstacles.' Thirdly, there is the example of the suffering of Jesus. As Stef puts it, 'God is a compassionate God who for our sake sent Christ to die on the cross, enduring immense suffering none of us can comprehend. Christ chose to endure this death for us in order that he could pay the price for all our wrongdoing and so we might be forgiven by God. I've learned that I might not enjoy suffering, but can find joy in it.' Fourthly, she accepts the limitations of what we can know now: 'There is lots I won't understand about God in this life, but I'm okay with it. It doesn't bother me. It's ridiculous to think my small human brain could understand everything about an infinite, all-powerful God. I know God is good and can redeem even the worst situation.'

After the accident Stef's sporting aspirations took a back seat and she explored new things, setting her heart on becoming a doctor. She was awarded an academic scholarship to study medicine at Queen's University in Ontario. However three weeks into her first term she went to watch the track and field athletes. Big mistake. Once bitten, forever smitten! Within days she was training with them, and four years of hard work later she was competing in her first international meet. It was her first taste of Paralympic sport and there was no turning back.

Her achievements as a Paralympic athlete since then, now competing for Great Britain, speak for themselves. To add to her honours degree in biochemistry, she has an impressive string of sporting honours and medals: five-time world-record holder in the long jump; triple Paralympic medallist in the long jump (2012, 2016) and 200m sprint (2008); and now reigning world champion in the long jump (London 2017 World Para Championships), having finally struck gold after over a decade of trying.

She was the poster girl for the London 2012 Paralympic Games but, like any athlete at her level, has had her ups and downs and battles with injury. In 2015 she was out for the season with a prolapsed disc. Then in early 2016 she developed a sore on her stump which meant she couldn't wear any artificial leg at all for 10 weeks. It was touch and go whether or not she would be able to start training again in time to compete at the Paralympics that year. But things came together at the eleventh hour, and that July she broke the long jump world record.

Sport is not only something Stef loves; she has learned from it too. She says, 'Sport is like a microcosm of life. You get to practice lots of things in a safe environment and then take them into real life.' Even so, some might question whether spending your life trying to jump a few centimetres further into a sandpit really is a worthwhile use of your remaining years on the planet. And they might wonder too how this fits in with Stef's re-evaluation, following the accident, of what really matters in the light of death and eternity. It has taken Stef a long time to gain clarity on the issue, not just in her head but in her heart, but this is the conclusion she has come to as a Christian:

God has honoured all of us with gifts and energy and talent. Part of my living out my life in worship to him is doing the best I can with every opportunity he has given me. I take that really seriously. At this point in my life God has called me to be an athlete. As long as he has called me to do this, I will do it to the best of my ability. That means striving to jump as far as I can. I am accountable to God for the quality of my work every day. Sport is my job, not just my recreation. It's how I connect with the world. It matters that I give everything I have.

So Stef does what she does for God, to the best of her ability, and leaves the results in his hands: 'I don't need to obsess over the outcome. I'm not afraid of failing. My identity is not tied to this. Growing up my whole identity did ride on results, and it was exhausting. I have peace and balance now.' Her Christian faith has also freed her to relate differently to her competitors. She goes on to explain,

Before, I didn't want to relate to them but just beat them, and I ignored them if they weren't doing well. But now

God has changed my heart, and I have a deep love and respect for my competitors. I want to stand with them, not on top of them. I know what they've gone through, and my worth is not dependent on them failing.

For Stef living differently is vitally important. She says 'If you are a Christian you don't need to carry a Bible around all the time or shout about it. It should be very obvious from how you do things. It should scream out that something is different about me.' But the place that living differently has can also be misunderstood, so a couple of qualifications are worth making. Firstly, in the light of death and eternity Stef is very aware that people need more than just to see a changed life. They need to hear the good news about Jesus, as she did. And so she is open about her faith in Christ, and makes the most of opportunities to share that with others.

And secondly, God does not accept Stef because she lives differently. It's the other way round. She is different because God has accepted her through Christ. The changed life is a fruit of God's grace at work in her. When it comes to leaping into sandpits Stef can jump further than most people, but there is a gap that she recognises even she couldn't jump, and that is the gap between us and God. The Bible says, 'all have sinned and fall short of the glory of God.' None of us lives the life we should. We all fail and fall short of God's standards. That is why we need Jesus. Through his death on the cross Jesus took the punishment that we deserve for our wrongdoing. Through him God himself has bridged the gap that separates all of us as sinful people from the holiness of God, and invites all who trust in Jesus to walk over to his side. Stef sums up this heart of the Christian message as 'Jesus did all the work and I get all the benefits'. However, that is not to say that the Christian life is then one of sitting back and doing nothing. On the contrary, the Bible likens the Christian life to a race in which we need to make every effort to persevere in faith and obedience. It's a metaphor that understandably resonates with Stef. She says, 'God calls his people to strive for the things of the kingdom. I'm going to strive as I hard as I can to live life for God's will, and love him better, and orient my mind and heart to him and his values.'

As for the future, Stef comments that before the accident she used to think heaven would be really boring. She doesn't now. What God promises his people in eternity is life in a renewed world with him and his people. All God's people will not only be raised to life but will have a perfect resurrection body. Jesus' resurrection from the dead is the guarantee and prototype of this. For someone like Stef, with only one leg, it is an appealing prospect, but not just for herself. She observes, 'Some things are annoying, like having to travel with four suitcases full of legs, but my disability is not as visible as that of others. And I'm mobile. For Brent, it's harder. I look forward to seeing him walking and running in heaven.' Brent is her wheelchair-racing husband – a world-record holder, seven-time Paralympic medallist, and seven-time world champion.

Stef and Brent often compete at the same meets. It can be difficult when one of them does well and the other doesn't. She remembers coming last in the long jump in 2013 and praying, 'God make me a big enough person to celebrate when he wins.' He did win, and she rejoiced with him.

Although Stef looks forward to life in eternity with a resurrection body, for now she has some more immediate goals demanding her attention. Her perspective after the London 2012 Paralympics was 'I'm totally in for the next one'. Now with Rio 2016 behind her the focus is all on 2020. The one Paralympic medal that still eludes her is gold. Bronze in 2008; silver in 2012 and 2016; gold in Tokyo? It would be a fairy-tale ending to her story, but she leaves it in God's hands. She knows God does not owe her or promise her success in return for living for him: 'It's easy to want to write your own destiny and story. But I trust God enough to let him do it his way. And my love for him is not tied in to the success he gives me. I will do the best I can.'

With a 2017 World Championship gold already round her neck, she knows how good that highest achievement feels, but she also has perspective: 'Winning gold is special, but it's not the be-all and end-all.' Her world won't come crashing down if she's not standing in the middle of the podium in Tokyo – but if she isn't, it won't be for lack of trying. As one feature article says about her, 'She is an example to us all. Her dedication and desire to fight back after losing in major events highlights an attitude that screams "try, try, and try again".' It's an attitude to loss forged in the fires of competition – and in the waters of a lake.

2

Rothschild Rainmaker
Akeel Sachak

Don't all religions lead to God?

When Akeel Sachak started out in the City as a young graduate, people would often be dismayed to learn that he was a committed Christian. As he explains,

> *There was the perception that a living Christian faith is not compatible with being a successful banker. The stereotype was that you could only succeed as a banker by being ruthless and unscrupulous. So many think that if you take God's Word seriously you must be soft in the head and can't be successful, because you need 'a crutch' to lean on.*

If people were tempted to dismiss Akeel because of his faith in those early days, they are less inclined to do so now 30 years on. His Christian faith is as strong as ever, his integrity is intact, and his rise to the top has been vertical. The man who is now known in the media as 'the Rothschild rainmaker' has proved the perception wrong.

Akeel joined the Rothschild investment bank back in the 1980s as a lowly number cruncher. He is now Global Head of Consumer, responsible for all the bank's activities in consumer products manufacturing, retail, luxury goods, hotels and restaurants. The sector he runs brought in a quarter of the bank's investment banking revenues this year. He is on the firm's global partnership management committee, but spends 90% of his time on deals, at which he's exceptionally good. One media article refers to him as 'dealmaker extraordinaire' and says, 'name any of this year's biggest grocery deals and chances are Akeel Sachak was involved. He is grocery's go-to guy when it comes to M&A [mergers and acquisitions] negotiations.'[1]

If 'grocery deals' makes you think of special offers and 'buy one, get one free' at the supermarket, think again. Think instead of the leading Japanese brewer, Asahi, last year buying $12 billion worth of European beer assets from Anheuser-Busch Inbev, which includes the Peroni, Grolsch, Pilsner Urquel, and Meantime brands. Or think of Shanghai-based Bright Food buying the entire Weetabix operation with a view to luring a billion Chinese away from their traditional breakfast of rice and steamed bread. Or think of a $30 billion deal merging all the Coca-Cola bottlers in Europe into a single company. This is what Akeel does. He brings the parties together, leads the negotiations, and makes these deals happen.

It's big business and it takes him all over the world. On average he's travelling two days a week, using the plane as his hotel room, and doing day trips to places as distant as Mexico City, Tokyo, and Sao Paolo. Comfortable as it may be in business class, especially when you're upgraded to first, as often happens, it's still a punishing schedule and he has to be available round the clock. The other week he took some time off to hike up Mt Kilimanjaro with his two sons yet had to take along a satellite phone so that clients could still get hold of him in the absence of mobile reception. But he loves what he does and sees it as part of how he serves God:

> The Bible tells us that God is a worker, and he has entrusted work to us made in his image as a God-given responsibility. He could have created a world in which we don't need to work, but he didn't. Work is part of what God wants us to do. Using our God-given abilities to serve him is one way we honour him. I have to remind myself not to compartmentalise my life into work and church. My whole life is to be given in service to God. I'm as much in full-time ministry as any full-time church worker.

Akeel sees the particular work he does as providing an important function in society and the economy, ensuring businesses are structured and operated as efficiently as possible.

If his heart for business runs in the family, his Christian faith definitely doesn't. Akeel's family are Indian, from Gujarat. His grandfather was a remarkable individual who started off as an immigrant to East Africa, selling animal hides, and then sold the business to buy farmland to plant sisal, the fibre of which is used to make rope and other products. He took control of the worldwide sisal industry for 40 years and made his fortune. Going back many generations Akeel's family have been Muslim. Islam is the faith he was born into and grew up in, but for him it was more a cultural badge than a personal belief: 'I would have said I believed in Allah, but I wouldn't have been able to articulate in any coherent way what I believed or the implications of belief. It just didn't engage me. I would recite bits of the Koran, but didn't understand a word of it.' Akeel would go to the mosque with his family on high days and holy days. He was the Muslim equivalent of the nominal Christian who attends church at Christmas and Easter. But it was as a student that all this was to change.

Akeel had always had ambition to excel. He had set his sights on studying law at Christ Church in Oxford, and that is what he did. For most of his three years as an undergraduate, God didn't really feature. He says, 'I had a superstitious belief in God, and would have recited some Muslim prayers if things got tough, but I didn't address my mind to God in any serious way. I had lots to distract me. Life was about having a good time, making friends, and getting by with academic study.' But then in his final term a fellow law student invited him to attend a Christian talk with her. He went along only because he thought she fancied him and was asking him out on a date! He remembers nothing of the talk, but it had a sufficient impact on him that he agreed to meet up with the speaker for a coffee. Over the course of several such meetings, and through his own reading of the gospel accounts in the Bible, he found his worldview being challenged at all sorts of levels. As he puts it,

I was confronted for the first time with the idea that not believing in God required more faith than believing in him. I began to understand the claims about God in the Bible, which was something to which I had not previously given a moment's thought, despite considering myself an intellectually inquisitive person. And the more I looked into those claims, the more I was persuaded of their truth. I am not sure how I ever imagined that there might be multiple legitimate faiths, when even a cursory examination of their respective claims made it clear they were mutually exclusive. Moreover I was struck that Jesus was a real historical figure, better authenticated than most before or since, including Mohammed.

But the biggest challenge to his thinking was regarding how a person gets right with God and relates to him:

My understanding of God had been about what I had to do, rather than what he had done for me. Growing up I viewed Jesus Christ as a good man at best for whom things had not turned out so well. The idea that God could enter his creation would have been extraordinarily demeaning. And I had no idea of personal relationship with God. That wouldn't have meant anything to me. But now I encountered a faith system that dealt with my real-world experience of human nature, and discovered that my relationship with God depended not on how good I could be, but entirely on what God has done for me. Most importantly I came to understand that Jesus was God entering his own creation.

What exactly God did through Jesus is something that Akeel grew to appreciate more and more over time:

I understood that I couldn't get myself out of my situation into relationship with God on my own. I depended entirely on God. And Jesus was essential if I was to enjoy a relationship with God. Jesus died instead of me. On the cross Jesus took on himself all I've done in terms of rebellion, and God's perfect justice was perfectly satisfied.

And so during these final weeks at Oxford the pieces of the jigsaw of the Christian faith started falling into place in his mind, and a coherent picture began to emerge which made sense and was convincing. But Akeel didn't act on it until meeting the speaker again one morning on his way into college to do some revision. It was then that he took the step of committing his life to Jesus Christ. He readily admits that his motives at the time were quite mixed, doing it partly because he knew it was what the speaker wanted and was a way of getting him off his back. But despite that, when a few weeks later he found himself standing dripping wet in the River Isis, having just been baptised by immersion, it was no formality but instead a real and life-changing new beginning. He was filled with excitement and enthusiasm, and overwhelmed with an enormous sense of relief – 'relief because I felt I had been denying a fundamental truth about life, God, myself, and how God engages with us. It made sense of everything that otherwise seemed incoherent.'

What had happened over that final term – moving from an unconsidered, superstitious view of Allah to a conviction that the biblical message about Jesus is true, and then to personal faith in Jesus Christ – is not something Akeel saw coming. He had just been getting on with life and doing well, and had not been searching for anything. Looking back, the only way he can make sense of what happened is that 'I wasn't searching for anything. God found me.'

It was only really after committing his life to Christ that the enormity of what he had done and the implications of it began to sink in. It was to make his life both easier and more difficult:

Life was more difficult because it changed the direction of my life in every way. My newfound faith was initially an inconvenient truth. It meant changing everything about the way I lived my life. And I actually went through a phase of trying to unbelieve what I believed – but without success.

Life was also more difficult because to speak about a living faith in Jesus as God and in his living Word is profoundly counter-cultural and eccentric in the financial world of the City.

But the biggest cost was in relationship with his family. He says, 'My parents read it as a profound rejection of them and their culture, rather than a rejection of Islam.' He remembers the reaction of his father when he told him – horrified, aggressive, and very angry. He adds, 'The passage of time has made it a bit easier, but I'm not sure my relationship with my parents has ever really recovered. Even now they struggle with it 30 years on. It means I have to live with a ruptured relationship with them.'

However in other ways faith in Christ has made life easier:

It has been easier because I have clarity about why I am in this world and where I am headed. I never have the desolation of asking, 'What's it all for?'

It's also been easier because it gives me a clear framework for living my life that hopefully helps me to be the kind of husband, father, son, friend, colleague, and banker that I should be. When honouring God is the catalyst for behaviour, the choices become a whole lot easier. Decision-making is easier because I am clear about what God expects of me in any given situation – how to think, where to go, what to do, how to do it.

Akeel would be the first to admit that he doesn't always walk the talk, and that he is very much a work in progress.

But his aim at least is 'to honour God with all I do, rather than honour and glorify myself'. The death of Jesus in the past and the promised return of Jesus in the future are the context within which he seeks to live:

> What I try to do is remind myself that I need to live in readiness for the return of Jesus every minute of every day and live constantly in the light of it. I'm here for God's purpose. I'm called on to be distinctive in how I handle myself in every area of life, doing everything in the name of Jesus.

That certainly includes his working life. Contrary to the stereotype of needing to be ruthless and unscrupulous to succeed in banking, he maintains that his long-standing relationships with clients are testament to the way he does business as a follower of Christ: 'In the 30 years I've been here, I've never been required to compromise my ethics or integrity in any way.' As a Christian he also seeks to be conscientious and committed in his work: 'My faith in God makes me want to be the best I can be in my work, for his glory, with the abilities with which he has blessed me.' Ultimately, as a Christian, his goal is to be like Christ: 'to reflect the image of Christ in the way I am in the workplace'. He adds, 'I will remain a sinful man until the new creation, when I am recreated fully in the image of Christ. But through God's grace and the transforming work of the Holy Spirit, I am different to what I was 30 years ago.'

One of the biggest thrills for Akeel in his work is getting a deal agreed that would not have happened without him, especially when the various parties involved recognise that. One of the things he does best is bringing people together, helping them understand the perspective of the other, and figuring out a way forward. In this respect his work could be seen in some small way as reflecting the work of Christ, the supreme mediator, who has brought about a reconciliation between two parties, sinful humanity and a holy God, that in human terms was impossible.

He is aware that what the Bible says, particularly about how to live, is increasingly seen as not just eccentric and irrelevant but also unacceptable to a rational person. But the message of what Christ has done for us is such good news that Akeel can't keep it to himself. He feels the responsibility to share it with others, however hard that may be. As he says,

> God has put me where I am for his purposes. I have a unique platform to witness and proclaim the gospel, and I need to be prepared to get up and do it. It's easier with clients than with colleagues, as it's a more equal relationship. I frequently have a Christian speaker at a dinner for clients at home, and it is extraordinary to see how the good news about Jesus touches them.

He is clear about the division of labour:

My role is to give others the opportunity to hear God's
Word, whether that is at church or at a dinner I am
hosting. It is not my job to convert people, but to get them
to hear the gospel – whether that is from me or a friend of
mine or a speaker I have invited for them to hear.

This longing to give as many as possible the opportunity
to hear the true message of the Bible shapes not just how
he relates to those he meets in his working life; it also
affects how he uses his financial resources as he seeks to
enable this good news to go out to others, both in this
country and overseas: 'Gospel proclamation meets the
most fundamental need of all of us, which is to be saved
for eternity. Anything that can help people hear the good
news of salvation through Jesus Christ is something I feel
I need to prioritise.'

So Akeel puts his money where his mouth is, partnering
with people all around the world who need resources to
carry out this work. It is a partnership with significant
historical precedent. The Bible translator William
Tyndale, for example, who pioneered the translation
of the Bible into English in the 16th century, could not
have done so without the financial backing of a wealthy
Christian businessman by the name of Humphrey
Monmouth, who made his fortune in the cloth business.
This is just one of many inspirational stories which
motivate the charity 'Gospel Patrons' with which Akeel
is involved. He explains, 'If you look back on the history
of gospel proclamation, you see this partnership between

proclaimers and those with resources like me. This is the model I want to fulfil.'

Putting his money to good use in this way is part of a wider attitude to money shaped by his Christian faith, and in particular by Bible passages such as 1 Timothy chapter 6 verses 17–19 which speak about how the rich are to use their resources. He articulates that,

> I don't see my wealth as independent of my faith or in conflict with it. Wealth is not a bad thing. It is a resource entrusted to me by God for his purpose and to enable his work. My wealth is God's wealth, for which I am a steward on his behalf. I have prospered because God has chosen to let me prosper, rather than any merit on my part. I am accountable to God at the end of the day for all the resources he has entrusted to me. So what I need to do is to master my wealth for God and not be mastered by it. That is a constant struggle, but the Bible tells us very clearly that we cannot serve two masters. We cannot serve God and money.

Akeel wouldn't claim to have this struggle all sorted by any stretch, and knows how hard it can be to strike a right balance between the enjoyment of God's good creation and the call to be radically generous, as God has been to us. This is something he keeps under constant review, knowing that time is short. As he points out, 'I'm 54 years old. I've only got a few years left doing what I'm doing with the resources and connectivity I enjoy. I need to respond to that challenge now.'

One newspaper feature article about Akeel refers to him as having 'the slicked-back hair that lends him the appearance of a 21st-century, multicultural version of Gordon Gekko'.[2] The comparison with the fictional financier played by Michael Douglas in the 1987 film *Wall Street*, who became a symbol for the 'Greed is Good' culture, could not be more inappropriate. Gekko's self-centred materialism is a world away from the 'Giving is Good' approach of this Rothschild rainmaker. People say, 'Don't judge a book by its cover'. We might add, 'And don't judge a banker by his hair!'

3

Premier League Footballer
Gavin Peacock

What is the purpose of life?

'Life and death. And between the two, football': those opening words from a book about the rivalry between Barcelona and Real Madrid – *Fear and Loathing in La Liga*[1] – describe what you find when you visit the Nou Camp, the home of Barcelona football club and Europe's largest stadium. On the one side there is a maternity hospital, and on the other a cemetery. But that physical reality also pictures how important football is for many people. It's what they live for. It's their god. It was Gavin Peacock's god too until one evening he was confronted by the true God, and his whole life changed.

Growing up in a footballing family, football was in his blood and the smell of the dressing room was in the air he breathed. His dad, Keith, played for Charlton Athletic for 17 years, notching up more games than any other outfield player in Charlton's history, and he went on to be the assistant manager at The Valley. He was also the first ever substitute in league football, an honour for which he is recognised in a Trivial Pursuit question. Following in his father's footsteps Gavin worked his way up through the ranks, playing for district, county, and then England Schoolboys. Aged 15 he played against Scotland at Wembley, with 65,000 watching in the stadium and millions more on TV. That was on a Saturday. On the Monday morning he was back to school to sit his Maths GCSE.

It was then that the big clubs came knocking on his door – Manchester United, Liverpool, Arsenal. But First Division club QPR, under their bright young manager, Terry Venables, looked like providing the quickest route to regular first-team football. So Gavin signed for them. At the age of 17 he had realised the schoolboy dream to play professional football. He had made it. He had it all – money, growing fame, and a great career ahead of him. But something was missing.

He says, 'I had achieved my goal. I had got to the top. I thought it would make me happy, but it didn't. Football was my god. When I played well I was up, but when I didn't I was down. It didn't satisfy. And I started questioning what the purpose of life was.' With this sense of dissatisfaction rumbling away inside, he decided one Sunday evening to check out the local church down the road. Until that point he hadn't given God much thought. His parents weren't Christian. He reckoned there was probably a God up there somewhere, but he comments, 'God had no bearing on my life at all, and I wasn't interested in what he said in the Bible. I wasn't doing drugs or sleeping around, and thought of myself as a moral, decent person.'

After the church service the minister invited him to a youth meeting back at his house. Gavin recalls,

> I walked into his front room having everything the world says will make you happy. I saw half a dozen people my age who had none of that. But when I heard them speaking about Jesus and praying, and when I saw the joy and reality in their lives, I realised they had something I didn't. And over the next few weeks I heard the message of the Bible – the good news of what God has done through Jesus to rescue us. I'd never heard it before. I became convinced Jesus was who he said he was and that I needed to turn around and trust in him.

There's a passage in the Bible which says, '… you turned to God from idols to serve the living and true God, and to wait for his Son from heaven, whom he raised from the dead – Jesus, who rescues us from the coming wrath.'[2] That is what Gavin did. He realised that football had been his idol, whereas the God who made everything is the one living and true God, and that we were made for him. Anything else we put in the centre circle of our lives – be it football, money, success, status, the approval of others – is a false god. We all do this, the Bible says, turning good things into god things. But these false gods cannot satisfy our deepest longings as human beings, and leaves us empty and unfulfilled. Not only that but they leave us on a collision course with our Creator, who will one day judge the world.

Gavin describes how he came to understand that God, being a just judge, cannot ignore our wrongdoing. Yet in his great mercy and love he sent his Son Jesus Christ to rescue us. Jesus lived the perfect life and died for us, taking on himself the punishment our wrongdoing deserves. He now offers forgiveness and eternal life to all who turn to him and trust in him. For those that do so a new life begins with the true God at the centre, back where he belongs in place of the false gods. Gavin explains, 'Ultimately it's about knowing God and being in a right relationship with him through Jesus. It's really freeing, because as a Christian you're not looking to your good works to be right with God. You're looking outside of yourself to another person, to Jesus, and his perfect life and death on the cross.'

The change was immediate. He says, 'Football had been my god. 100%. Now it fell into its right place. It wasn't god any more. Jesus was central. Your whole life and motivation for what you do changes.' It shaped life on the field as well as off. He continues, 'Whatever we do we are to do it for God. So I now saw my football gifts as from God and for his glory. And I actually played better, because my identity was not in football. I was more relaxed as a player.' It also brought a different perspective to the ups and downs: 'In football you can be a hero on Saturday, and then a zero on Tuesday when you miss an open goal and get injured. But Jesus brings perspective and by the Holy Spirit he is with you.'

Inevitably Gavin faced his fair share of mickey-taking as word got round that he had become 'a born-again Christian'. But spending 10 months of the year living with a bunch of men gave plenty of opportunity for them to see that there was an authenticity and integrity not just in what he said but in how he lived, albeit imperfectly. However, bigger tests of his new-found Christian faith were to come.

The first challenge was being relegated. Twice. Impatient to play regular first-team football, he had moved to Third Division Gillingham, where his father was manager. The season ended in relegation. He then moved to First Division Bournemouth to play under up-and-coming young manager Harry Redknapp. That season also ended in them going down. Two relegations in two years was a bitter pill so early in Gavin's career. But he comments,

> *That you've become a Christian doesn't mean everything is going to go well in life. Because my identity was not tied up in football it meant I could ride the ups and downs with equilibrium. My focus was on Jesus. And knowing that my best life was not now but to come in eternity, that hope of heaven, gives confidence to live through difficult times now. And such trials can strengthen your faith, and you can have joy even when everything around you is moving.*

As it happened things were about to start moving in a better direction. Harry Redknapp was always on his phone during training – the lads used to joke that he was placing bets on the dogs and horses – and one day he came over to Gavin having just taken a call from another club. 'Newcastle are coming for you,' he said. Gavin had only been married a year and they'd just got settled into life in Bournemouth, but he knew he had no choice. 'It's a big club,' he told his wife when he got home. 'We've got to go.' She burst into tears, yet this was the moment when Gavin's career took off.

At Newcastle he played first under Jim Smith, and then under Ossie Ardiles, the 1978 World Cup winner with Argentina and Maradona's mentor. But it was under Ardiles's successor that the fortunes of the club rocketed. Gavin remembers hearing on the radio, as he drove over the Tyne Bridge, the news that Newcastle had appointed Kevin Keegan as their new manager. Keegan was seen as the messiah coming to save the club. He didn't disappoint. Gavin says, 'He was a great visionary, and a great man-manager and motivator.'

Gavin remembers Keegan's first game in charge. Keegan went round the dressing room, speaking to each of the guys in turn. He got to Gavin, looked at him, and said, 'You're the man. You're the one today. Bill Shankley used to say to me, "Just go out there and drop hand grenades all over the field." That's you now. You're the danger man.' Gavin recalls thinking, 'Shankley was a legend as manager at Liverpool. And he'd treated Keegan as a son. And now Keegan, my hero, was treating me like a son, saying to me what Shankley said to him.' Gavin was so fired up he burst out of the tunnel and Newcastle won 3-0. A couple of years later, when Keegan was given the England job, Paul Scholes scored a hat trick in their match against Poland and afterwards praised Keegan's role as a motivator. Scholes, a midfielder like Gavin, said the next day, 'Before the match, in the dressing room, Keegan came up to me and said, "Bill Shankley used to say to me …!"'

Being a Christian shaped Gavin's attitude to both winning and losing. He says, 'Within the rules of the game I'd do what I could to beat you and score, because that was my job. And I'd run all day. The game demanded that I was competitive. And I was disappointed when we lost. But winning wasn't everything to me. Jesus was more important. I had what really matters in life.' That first season at Newcastle ended with promotion to the Premier League and with the team riding around the city centre in an open-top bus parade, the streets lined with fans. But the high was quickly followed by another challenge two weeks later.

His wife Amanda was pregnant with their first child. After a difficult labour Jake was born. It was only as the baby cried and stretched out his arms that they realised a third of his right arm was missing. It was a complete shock. Little was known at the time about limb deficiency and the immediate concern was that there might be other problems too. But ironically the doctor, who wasn't a Christian, said to them 'This is the body God has given Jake.' He expressed what they believed and what gave them a rock on which to stand. Gavin states, 'We knew that God is in control of all things, and that Jake was okay and was in his hands.' Their son went on to compete at international level in martial arts and has just opened his own gym.

Ups and downs were to characterise Gavin's first season at his next club. This move took him back down south – to Chelsea – for £1.25m. In his Chelsea years he was to play alongside some great players – Dennis Wise, Tony Cascarino, Gianfranco Zola, Ruud Gullit, Gianluca Vialli. But he says the best player he ever played with was Glenn Hoddle, the player-manager when Gavin joined the club. Keegan had told Gavin that he would learn more from playing with Hoddle than from anyone else. He was right. Eric Cantona of Manchester United said of him after a game, 'Hoddle was like Mozart in a world of heavy rockers.'

It was against Manchester United that Gavin made his mark in his first season at Chelsea. He scored the only goal in the game against them at Stamford Bridge. Then in March they headed up to Old Trafford to face United on their home turf. It was a daunting prospect. The 1993–94 United team line-up included the likes of Ryan Giggs, Eric Cantona, Mark Hughes, Andrei Kanchelskis, Roy Keane, and Peter Schmeichel. Gavin remembers one moment in the game when the ball bounced a few metres in front of him in the box. He thought, 'If only I can just get there before Schmeichel.' He did get his boot to it just before he felt the great Dane's studs in his thigh. The ball headed for the line and rolled over before Steve Bruce could stop it. Chelsea won 1-0 again. They'd done the double over United, Gavin scoring both times. Of the more than 100 goals he scored in his 18-year professional career and 600 games, these were two of the sweetest.

United went on to win the league, but the teams were to do battle again at the end of the season, this time on the biggest stage of all – at Wembley for the FA Cup Final. The atmosphere was electric. 100,000 crammed into the stadium. Millions were watching on TV. It was red versus blue, north versus south. Gavin remembers the roar as he came out of the tunnel. Even during the game he could hardly hear the player next to him. He can still replay in his mind's eye the volley he struck in the first half: 'It just flew off my boot. Schmeichel was backpedalling. Everything went into slow motion. It sailed over his head. It was going in. It hit the crossbar. And out it came. And everything went back to normal speed. An inch can make the difference between success and failure.' They went in at half-time level at 0-0.

Hoddle's words, 'Don't do anything silly early in the second half', were still ringing in Chelsea's ears when they gave away a penalty. Cantona swaggered up and placed the ball on the spot. Little Dennis Wise went up to him and tried to put him off: '£50 says you miss,' he said. Big Eric didn't even bother to reply. He checked his trademark turned-up collar was still in place, strolled up to the ball, and stroked it past the goalkeeper. Minutes later there was another penalty, albeit a mistake by the referee, so Gavin claims. Cantona stepped up again. This time he strolled over to Dennis, looked down at him, and said in his thick French accent, 'Double or nothing'. He sauntered back to the spot. Same side. Bottom corner. 2-0. Gavin rates Cantona as the best player he ever played against: 'He was king. Strong. Fast. Phenomenal ability. Invincible confidence on the field.' Chelsea lost the final 4-0.

Gavin's teammate John Spencer was so distraught he threw his runners-up medal into the Thames. For Spencer football was everything. Gavin knew him well and had tried to share a Christian perspective with him over the years, but Spencer had wanted nothing to do with it. When the club chaplain came round he would be the guy trying to crawl out, warning, 'The vicar's in the room.' Just recently though, almost 25 years on, Gavin received a text from him out of the blue saying, 'You'll never guess what! I'm now reading the Bible and going to church.' He had come to see his own need of being in a right relationship with God through Jesus and had started following him.

Gavin finished his playing career back at QPR, and then began a second dream career working for the BBC as a football pundit and commentator. He started by covering the Africa Cup of Nations with Garth Crooks. Then he moved on to *Football Focus, Match of the Day*, and *MOTD2*. He spent six years working alongside people like Gary Lineker, Ian Wright, Alan Hansen, Lee Dixon, and Alan Shearer. Gavin remarks, 'They were all internationals who had achieved far more than me on the field, so I had to make sure I was good at what I did, giving people at home an insight into the game.'

At this point in the early 2000s, being on the screen every week meant he was more famous than he'd ever been as a player. Things could not have been going better and he loved what he did. But he had a deepening conviction that God now wanted him to serve him in a very different way – as a church pastor. He refers to his growing desire at the time to teach the Bible and preach the gospel as 'a joyful compulsion'. This sense he had was tested and affirmed by church leaders. He started some biblical studies. And then the day came when he did his final programme with the BBC and announced that he was leaving for Canada to serve as a pastor.

It was a huge change, stepping out of the media glare into the obscurity and anonymity of a small town in Calgary. His football debut on the pitch had been in front of 15,000; his preaching debut in the pulpit was in front of 15. It was a difficult but deliberate step. He understands, 'God needed to do a work in me and humble me. He could do this best out of the limelight.' It's now nine years since he and his family moved there. He says they've been the most difficult years of his life, but he loves what he does and knows they are where God wants them to be. Does he miss football? He answers, 'I miss being super fit, and being with the lads in the dressing room. But because my identity was not in it, I could move on. Football is just for a few years, but Jesus is for ever. When football is gone, Jesus is still there.'

He turns 50 this year and is very conscious of how quickly time passes. But it doesn't faze him. He explains,

As a Christian every day is one day closer to heaven. The apostle Paul said, '… to me, to live is Christ and to die is gain.'[3] It's a win-win for the Christian. We live for Christ now, and when we die we go to be with Christ for ever. And even now, as our bodies start to go south, inside we're being strengthened as our hope gets stronger.

What would he like as the epitaph on his tombstone? He thinks for a moment, smiles, and replies, 'Football is great. But Jesus is greater.'

4

Oxford Professor
John Lennox

Hasn't science disproved God?

The report in *The Wall Street Journal* began, 'The event had been sold out for weeks. Tickets were being offered on the black market for three times their face value. With 30 minutes to showtime, the crowds were forming outside, some wolfing down sandwiches in the parking lot. For this much excitement, people around here generally expect some serious football.'[1] But for once the buzz had nothing to do with sport. The event in Alabama in 2007 was actually a debate on the existence of God, but this was no run-of-the-mill discussion. This was the academic equivalent of a boxing world-title fight between two heavyweight champions, with biologist Richard Dawkins in one corner and mathematician John Lennox in the other. Two Oxford professors in their 60s, an atheist and a Christian, both at the peak of their intellectual game, were going head to head, slugging it out in the ring.

Dawkins was by this stage already a well-known public intellectual with a global reputation – the passionate, aggressive spokesman of the atheist cause, a popular speaker, and bestselling author of *The Selfish Gene*[2] and *The God Delusion*.[3] 3 million copies of *The God Delusion* have been sold in English alone and it was the subject of the Alabama debate. The gentle, eloquent Lennox was by contrast little known beyond his academic circles. But this debate was to change that. Even if Dawkins was not knocked out, by the end he was certainly reeling from some heavy punches by the mild-mannered Irishman. Lennox's impressive performance was to catapult him on to the world stage. A rematch followed a year later, in Oxford's Museum of Natural History, on 'Has Science Buried God?', which was to become the subtitle of a bestselling book Lennox went on to write: *God's Undertaker*.[4] All of a sudden, he was the man to fight. He debated Christopher Hitchens on 'The New Atheism' and on 'Is God Great?', and Peter Singer on 'Is there a God?' as well as taking part in countless public discussions with other academics around the world.

The timing of this sudden burst of activity is no accident. Lennox begins his book *Gunning for God* with these words: 'Atheism is on the march in the Western world. Noisily. A concerted attempt is being made to marshal the atheist faithful, to encourage them not to be ashamed of their atheism but to stand up and fight as a united army. The enemy is God. They are gunning for God.'[5] As a result of this campaign by the New Atheists, Lennox says that 'the widespread belief is that atheism is "the automatic default position for all thinking people who hold science in high regard."[6] He is determined to challenge this in the public square and show otherwise.

As he goes about his task he is, in the words of John Horgan, one of his debating opponents, 'disarmingly genial'. Horgan continued, 'Lennox wins over many people by appealing to their hearts as well as intellects. Lennox loves God, loves the world, loves people – even atheists.' That's quite a testimony from an agnostic. It is this love that drives Lennox in his mission to defend Christianity against the atheistic objections, to present detailed evidence for the truth of Christianity, and to expose the flaws in the atheistic worldview.

The public battle in which he is now engaged is something for which his upbringing prepared him well. Lennox grew up in the small town of Armagh in Northern Ireland in a Christian home. He says, 'There was never a time when I denied the gospel, but it was clear to me that you become a Christian and are not born one. So somewhere along the line that trust developed into something real.'[7] His parents were committed Christians but not sectarian, which in that deeply divided culture was very unusual. His father ran a department store employing some 40 people, and did so across the religious divide. It was a brave and costly stand to take, and left a lasting impression on the young Lennox: 'My father had the deep conviction that all people were made in the image of God. His Christianity came across as really genuine.'

His parents were not only people of integrity and Christian character. They also had an open-minded intellectual curiosity and commitment to learning which was highly unusual in that culture. Lennox explains,

> My parents encouraged me to think. For me Christianity in my youth was associated with learning, not closed-mindedness. Christianity was open-ended and people were always discussing. I did a lot of reading and thinking. I had read almost all of C. S. Lewis before university, and vast numbers of other Christian books. But my father also encouraged me to read secular books.

He recalls his dad giving him a copy of Karl Marx's *Communist Manifesto* to read. When Lennox asked why he should bother he was told, 'You need to know what others think.'

As a result by the time he arrived in Cambridge as an undergraduate he was ready for battle, nailing his colours to the mast in the public square. Needless to say he initially encountered what he calls 'the Freudian challenge', namely that 'you believe because you are Irish'. But, he says, 'That is nonsensical because you can apply the same to atheism. It doesn't get you anywhere.' He loved the opportunity to dialogue with people who didn't share his worldview, firmly convinced that Christianity has real answers. One agnostic did become a Christian after two years of discussion. Lennox comments, 'It showed me that people can change their worldview.' It was for Lennox the beginning of a lifetime of dialogue.

Although he loves the exchange of ideas, it is not just an intellectual exercise. He sees what is at stake:

If you are an atheist and I am a Christian that will make a huge difference in the way we approach the big questions of life. What value has a human being, for example? I believe a human being is made in the image of God, and therefore of infinite value. But if you believe that a human being is just a being thrown up by some mindless naturalistic process, you are not going to have the same value, especially when it comes to unborn human beings. So ideas have consequences. The second thing is consequences for morality. We are in a crisis in Europe and the West because we do not know anymore where morality comes from.

In his dialogue over the years he has been confronted by two main objections to Christianity. Firstly that it is irrational, and secondly that it is immoral. The case for the second objection was enthusiastically argued by both Dawkins and the late Christopher Hitchens. Lennox responded in his book *Gunning for God*.

The accusation that religion is harmful and 'poisons everything', as Hitchens put it, is one that is close to home for Lennox, having grown up in Northern Ireland. His father's open-minded employment policy led to their family store being bombed several times, on one occasion causing one of his brothers to lose an eye and need 300 stitches to repair his face. But when the New Atheists tar Christianity with this brush, Lennox says, 'They inexcusably confuse the evils of renegade Christendom with the teachings of Christ, and thus think violence is part of the Christian faith; whereas the Christian faith itself actually explicitly repudiates violence.'[8] He argues that they also misrepresent the extent of the violence, and display 'culpable ignorance' of 'the great good that has been done throughout the centuries by those who genuinely follow Christ'.[9] In turn he states that they conveniently ignore the evils perpetrated by individuals such as Stalin, Mao, Hitler, and Pol Pot.

Lennox has travelled extensively in the former communist world and quotes Polish friends who say, 'Dawkins has lost contact with the realities of twentieth-century history. Let him come here and talk to us, if he is really open to listening to evidence of the link between atheism and atrocity.' Lennox's book goes on to look at a range of moral questions, including, 'Can we be good without God?' and, 'Is the God of the Bible a despot?'

Most of his work though has been devoted to addressing the first objection, namely that Christianity is irrational, particularly the claim that science and belief in God are in conflict. Even as a young boy Lennox came across the idea through C. S. Lewis that, far from there being a conflict, Christianity was actually responsible for the meteoric rise of science in the sixteenth and seventeenth centuries. Lewis writes, 'Men became scientific because they expected law in nature, and they expected law in nature because they believed in a lawgiver.'[10] Lennox adds, 'It is no accident that

Galileo, Kepler, Newton, and Clerk Maxwell were believers in God … Belief in God, far from hindering science, was the motor that drove it.' So many top-level scientists since and today share their Christian faith that Lennox says the conflict view is now 'discredited'. He goes on, 'There is real conflict, but it is not science versus religion. It is theism versus atheism, and there are scientists on both sides.'[11] It is this worldview question that is central to his book *God's Undertaker*. As he asks in the preface, 'Which worldview sits most comfortably with science – theism or atheism? Has science buried God or not? Let us see where the evidence leads.'[12]

He finds that this appeal to follow the evidence comes as a surprise to many, because they have swallowed the misconception that Christian faith is blind and means believing in the absence of evidence. He points out, 'It obscures the fact that faith in the New Testament is evidence-based, and that faith is actually also essential in science. You cannot do science unless you believe that science can be done.' He says that the blind faith label the New Atheists put on Christians can actually be 'a very convenient way of avoiding intelligent discussion about real evidence.'[13] It is on this evidence that Lennox wants to put the focus, and there is no shortage of it across the scientific disciplines, starting with Lennox's own field of expertise, namely mathematics.

He explains, 'As a child I was very fast at doing arithmetic. At primary school I would ask for extra homework in maths. I didn't find it difficult and had a good maths teacher.' The natural talent and interest he displayed in childhood was to become a lifelong passion. The long list of his academic qualifications, awards and achievements speaks for itself – MA and PhD in maths (plus an honorary MMath) at Cambridge University; DSc at University of Wales; MA in bioethics at University of Surrey; Professor of Maths at Oxford; over seventy published mathematical papers to his name; and the co-author of two research-level texts in algebra. One thing he loves about the subject is 'the precision and logic of maths'. He states, 'It is the tightest form of logic.' The discipline of logical analysis has stood him in good stead in battling the New Atheists of this world and focusing on 'the logic of the argument'.

Lennox is also fascinated by how maths points to God. He writes, 'For me as a mathematician the very mathematical intelligibility of the world, and the subtlety and power of the mathematics developed to describe it, constitute major evidences for the existence of a Creator'.[14] He asks, 'How is it that equations created in the head of a mathematician can relate to the universe outside that head? This question prompted Albert Einstein to say, "The only incomprehensible thing about the universe is that it is comprehensible."' Lennox quotes an essay by Eugene Wigner titled The Unreasonable Effectiveness Of Mathematics in which he writes, 'The enormous usefulness of mathematics in the natural sciences is something bordering on the mysterious, and there is no rational explanation for it'[15] – no explanation, that is, if you believe there is no God.

In the 17th century the mathematician and astronomer Johannes Kepler worked out from his maths and observation that the planets moved around the sun in perfect ellipses, not in circles as had been previously assumed. Isaac Newton then succeeded in getting that down to a mathematical equation: the law of gravity. He was so moved by this that he wrote the most brilliant book in the history of science, his *Principia Mathematica*, expressing the hope that it would persuade the thinking reader to believe in a Creator. Lennox shares this sense of wonder that, as he puts it, 'You can deduce all the motions of the planets from an equation with eight symbols in.'

This tradition of mathematicians peering through telescopes and marvelling at the beauty and mathematical intelligibility of what they see is one that Lennox himself is continuing. On a cold, clear winter's night he is often to be found in his tiny two-metre diameter observatory in his back garden, looking through his 10-inch telescope at the moon or Jupiter, or the Andromeda Galaxy with its 100 billion stars 2.5 million light years away. As a boy he visited the observatory in Armagh and asked the director what he feels as he looks at the night sky and whether he thinks there's a God. The man replied, 'I cannot look night after night and not think there's something more. There's the sense of something bigger. And the longing.'

But one of the most striking features of the universe that has come to light through contemporary science, and which points to a Creator, is its remarkable fine-tuning. The picture that has been emerging is, Lennox writes, one of 'a universe whose fundamental forces are amazingly, intricately, and delicately balanced or "fine-tuned" in order for the universe to be able to sustain life … Change any of them just a little, and the universe would become hostile to life and incapable of supporting it.'[16] He quotes eminent mathematician and astronomer Fred Hoyle, who confessed that nothing had shaken his atheism as much as the fact that many of the constants of nature have just the right values for life to exist. Hoyle said that it looked as if 'a superintellect has monkeyed with the physics as well as with chemistry and biology'.

The kind of accuracy needed even for just one aspect of this fine-tuning has been likened to that which 'a marksman would need to hit a coin at the far side of the observable universe, twenty billion light years away'.[17] Another illustration Lennox quotes, this time by an astrophysicist, Hugh Ross, puts it this way:

> *Cover America with coins in a column reaching to the moon, then do the same for a billion other continents of the same size. Paint one coin red and put it somewhere in one of the billion piles. Blindfold a friend and ask her to pick it out.*[18]

These are the kind of odds involved in such fine-tuning being the result of chance.

Hawking's answer to this fine-tuning is the 'multiverse' theory of there being many different universes. Lennox devotes a chapter in his book *God and Stephen Hawking* to refuting it (and Hawking's related 'M-theory'). He sums up by saying,

> *A move to advance the cause of atheism by means of a highly speculative, untestable theory that is not within the zone of evidence-based science, and which, even if it were true, could not dislodge God in any case, is not exactly calculated to impress those of us whose faith in God is not speculative but testable and well within the zone of evidence-based rational thought.*[19]

Another relatively recent discovery about the universe that points to God, Lennox adds, is the fact that it actually had a beginning, rather than eternally existing. The Big Bang may be widely accepted now, but when it was first proposed in the 1960s many struggled to accept it because of the implications. Lennox quotes Stephen Hawking, who acknowledges, 'Many people do not like the idea that time has a beginning, probably because it smacks of divine intervention.'[20] It confirms what the Bible has been saying all along, whereas the atheist is left struggling to explain where the universe has come from and why there is something rather than nothing. The best that the Cambridge theoretical physicist Stephen Hawking could come up with is, 'Because there is a law of gravity, the universe can and will create itself out of nothing.'[21] This is one of the main conclusions of Hawking's latest book, *The Grand Design*.[22] One of the refreshing things about Lennox is that he is not in the least intimidated by the likes of Hawking, despite describing him as 'the world's most famous living scientist'.[23]

In *God and Stephen Hawking* Lennox exposes the logical flaws that run through Hawking's argument, and manages to do so in an accessible way. For example, by likening the universe to a jet engine he illustrates how absurd it is for Hawking to ascribe creative powers to physical laws: 'The laws of physics can explain how the jet engine works, but not how it came to exist in the first place. It is self-evident that the laws of physics could not have created a jet engine on their own. The task also needed the intelligence, imagination, and scientific creativity of Whittle,'[24] referring to its inventor, Sir Frank Whittle.

Not only are the laws of physics incapable of creating anything, Lennox demonstrates that they cannot even cause anything to happen: 'Newton's celebrated laws of motion never caused a pool ball to race across the green baize table. That can only be done by people using a pool cue and the actions of their own muscles. The laws enable us to analyse the motion ... but they are powerless to move the ball, let alone bring it into existence.'[25] Lennox does not pull his punches in his assessment: 'Nonsense remains nonsense, even when talked about by world-famous scientists ... Immense prestige and authority does not compensate for faulty logic.'[26]

The atheist's difficulty of accounting for the scientific evidence becomes even more of an uphill struggle when you turn to the existence and complexity of life on earth.

It is here perhaps more than anywhere that the Creator has 'left his fingerprints all over his creation,'[27] as Lennox puts it. When Lennox is not in his mini observatory with a telescope he may well be found indulging his love of optical equipment with a pair of binoculars and a camera, while out birdwatching with his wife. What he sees, he says, is just what Darwin saw when he studied his finches all those years ago on the Galapagos Islands – variation and change. He comments, 'What Darwin observed is utterly uncontroversial.' But, and it is a very big 'but', he goes on to make clear: 'When it comes to extrapolation to vast shifts in body plans and organisms, the evidence simply isn't there. I'm not convinced as a scientist.

He is not alone in this. The question 'What is the evidence that random mutation and natural selection can bear the weight put on them?' is a big scientific one. He acknowledges, 'It is currently the majority belief in the biological community,' but adds, 'There is a lot of evidence in the other direction.' It's a topic he addresses at length in *God's Undertaker*, although aware from history of the difficulty facing those who question the accepted scientific view. The opposition to Kepler and Galileo in their day, when they produced evidence which went against the accepted Aristotelean view of the universe, bears witness to how readily evidence is dismissed which doesn't fit into the accepted box. The problem in the current situation, as Lennox sees it, is that if you are operating from an atheistic worldview, 'then macro-evolution is a logical necessity'. If you rule out a Creator, how else can you account for the existence and complexity of life? But both aspects present huge challenges to atheism.

The complexity of the living world has now been revealed as never before through molecular biology. Lennox quotes a geneticist, Michael Denton, who says that even the tiniest of bacterial cells, weighing less than a trillionth of a gram, is 'a veritable microminiaturized factory containing thousands of exquisitely designed pieces of intricate molecular machinery, made up altogether of 100,000 million atoms, far more complicated that any machine built by man.'[28] He illustrates this with the example given by the biochemist Michael Behe of 'the tiny acid-driven motor ... that powers the bacterial flagellum – a propeller-like device that enables bacteria to swim', and, which 'consists of some forty protein parts', the absence of any of which 'would result in complete loss of motor function'. Lennox says this 'irreducible complexity' presents a formidable challenge to evolutionary theory, 'as Darwin himself saw when he wrote that "If it could be demonstrated ... my theory would absolutely break down."'[29]

Another example is that of amino acids, which he calls 'the basic building blocks of living systems'[30] and from which proteins are made. There are 20 of them in living organisms and they have to be ordered in just the right way. The probability of getting them in the right order by chance, Lennox points out, was famously likened by Sir Fred Hoyle to 'the chance of a tornado sweeping through a junkyard and producing a Boeing 747 jet aircraft'.[31] That is even before you get to the question of how they arose in the first place.

The origin of this highly ordered complexity in biology poses a big challenge to atheism, but Lennox argues that the biggest is the origin of information in the living cell. He describes himself as 'a scientist deeply interested in language'. As a teenager he loved modern languages, but he couldn't afford to travel to learn them. Instead, at the age of 13, he built himself his own radio transmitter and became an amateur radio operator so he could talk to people around the world and learn languages that way. I Ie says that now anything hc can do in English he can do in German. His French and Russian are a bit behind, but he can still lecture in them in maths. He also has some Spanish. Yet his linguistic interest connects not just with his own learning of languages, but with the discovery of language-like information in DNA. He describes as one of the greatest scientific discoveries of all time that 'in each of the ten trillion cells of our body we humans possess a "word" of mind-boggling length, the human genome. This "word" is 3.5 billion "letters" long, written in the four chemical "letters" C, G, A, T.'[32]

Thc significance of this linguistic complexity at the heart of the living ccll, hc says, is that when we come across language we always deduce that a mind, an intelligence, must be behind it. He continues, 'We instinctively infer "upwards" to an ultimately intelligent causation rather than "downwards" to chance and necessity.'[33] He gives the example of an archaeologist finding on the walls of a hitherto unexplored cave two scratch marks which form the Chinese character for a human being. He comments, 'Is it not to be wondered at that our archaeologist immediately infers intelligent origin when faced with two scratches, whereas some scientists, when faced with the 3.5 billion letter sequence of the human genome, inform us that it is to be explained solely in terms of chance and necessity?'[34]

One such scientist is Dawkins. He uses the analogy of monkeys with typewriters to argue that, given enough time, a blind, mindless, unguided process has the power to produce biological information. Lennox devotes a whole chapter of God's Undertaker to this claim and shows it to be 'mathematical nonsense'[35] which only works by introducing 'two mechanisms, each of which bears every evidence of the input of an intelligent mind'.[36] He concludes: 'Dawkin's model is useless as a simulation of how complexity, in the sense of getting the letters in the right order, can be built from a random sequence by an undirected evolutionary process.'[37]

In summary Lennox's contention is that the results of science, and the very fact that we can do science, provide convincing 'evidence that there is a Mind behind the universe'.[38] But he is not content to leave things there. He asks, 'Is there any serious and credible evidence that the Mind has ever spoken into our world ... directly, as distinct from what we can learn of him indirectly through the structures of the universe?'[39] The biblical claim is that 'at a certain time and place God the Creator encoded himself in humanity'[40] in the person of Jesus Christ. This is the supreme evidence for God.

Although it takes us outside the realm of science into history, Lennox says the method we use to assess such a claim – what is called 'inference to the best explanation' – is the same that science uses for anything that is an unrepeatable past event, such as the origin of the universe or of life. The key question to consider is 'Did Jesus rise from the dead?' and this is the subject of the final chapter of *Gunning for God.*[41] His conclusion is: 'The evidence of the empty tomb, the character of the witnesses, the explosion of Christianity out of Judaism, and the testimony of millions today are inexplicable without the resurrection.'

His reference to the experience of people today is a strand of evidence for God that he says makes Christianity testable and should not be overlooked:

When you see people whose lives are in a mess (say through drug or alcohol addiction) and their case seems hopeless, and then you meet them six months later and their addiction has been changed to food on the table and they're happy and in restored relationships, and you ask them what's happened, and they say they have met Christ, and when you see that many times, two plus two in the end makes four. You realise that this is evidence that what Christ promised is true.

He elaborates in *God and Stephen Hawking*: 'I wish to add my voice to the many millions who can testify to the profound and central role that faith in Christ as Lord has on our lives, bringing assurance of peace with God, a new power for living, and a certain hope based on the resurrection of Christ.'[42] This transforming power is something he does not see in atheism. He issues this challenge: 'Let's meet here again in a year's time, and you bring me 10 people whose lives have been transformed by atheism, and I'll bring you 500 whose lives have been transformed by Christ.'

Lennox, like so many of us, is aware of 'the constant pressure to achieve' in life. It is a pressure, he says, that 'turns some people into workaholics, driven by an unreachable goal of that achievement that would give them, they hope, some enduring significance'.[43] But this pressure can also make it hard to grasp the Christian message. He writes,

> At the heart of Christianity is a willingness to trust Jesus Christ as Lord and Saviour and thereby receive forgiveness and peace with God ... The problem is that, in a world where achievement and merit count for so much, we human beings find it difficult to understand and accept that God's forgiveness and peace cannot be earned by our work, effort, or merit, but must be received as a free gift.[44]

We simply need to 'rest on the work that Christ has done – not on the work we do'.[45]

In the end what Lennox is advocating is 'an intelligent faith that is based on the cumulative evidence of science, history, the biblical narrative, and personal experience'.[46] This is the kind of faith that he not only promotes, but also embraces and embodies personally. It is anything but blind. In fact his contention is: 'the New Atheism is a belief system which, ironically, provides a classic example of the blind faith it so vocally despises in others'.[47] It is a provocative charge for which he gives compelling evidence that is worth taking seriously and examining further. For those who won't get to meet the genial Irishman in the ring, his material in books and online is a great place to start. But a word of warning: beware the left hook!

5

Bank CEO
Jeremy Marshall

What hope is there in the face of death?

Jeremy Marshall has experienced the best of times and the worst of times. He knows the feeling of power, sitting at an executive desk on the top floor of a bank as CEO, and the powerlessness of lying on a hospital trolley as a chemotherapy patient. He has known life in the fast lane of a career in international finance, and life in the lay-by, broken down and out of work. He has enjoyed the sunshine of earning more than many of us will see in a lifetime, and endured the storm of a terminal diagnosis that no amount of money can change. He's been waited on in board rooms, and been bored in waiting rooms. He's known the stress of long hours in the bank with too much to do, and the stress of long hours at the hospital with nothing to do. He's had the thrill of the view from the top of the tower, setting the vision for a banking business in strategic planning, and the terror of sitting alone in the darkness at the bottom of the pit, having lost his eyesight.

He knows what it's like to be on one side of the desk telling someone, 'You've had it; your job is over,' and to be on the other side listening to a consultant tell him, 'You've had it; you've got 18 months to live.' But the constant throughout this rollercoaster ride has been his faith in Jesus Christ. It is a faith that has given him strength in life and now gives him hope in the face of death.

As a child Jeremy didn't have much choice about going to church; his father was the local minister. But by the time he was in his teens he resisted it and dismissed it as a boring waste of time, until he came across some Russians who made him start to wonder if there was more to it all. His parents' idea of a fun family summer holiday every year was to pack him and his three young sisters into their old Austin 1800 to drive across Europe, visiting Christians in the Soviet Union and smuggling Bibles in behind the Iron Curtain. On these annual adventures Jeremy met Christians who had every reason not to believe. The prevailing communism there said that religion was just for the *babushkas*, the old women. If you didn't join the Communist Party you were harassed, couldn't go to university, and could be beaten up. Church pastors often found themselves in labour camps. Yet so many ordinary people Jeremy met did believe and lived out their faith with a radiant, joyful generosity and hospitality.

Then one day the penny dropped. Jeremy realised that Christianity isn't about religion but relationship. He says, 'It struck me that it was all about Jesus Christ, who really was the Son of God. That he really had lived and had died and had been raised to life, and really was alive today and could be known personally.' And so Jeremy came to a personal, living faith in a living Jesus. He went on to study history at Cambridge and became increasingly convinced that faith was not a blind leap in the dark, but was reasonable and logical. He quotes the maxim of Sherlock Holmes: 'When you have eliminated the impossible, whatever remains, however improbable, must be the truth.' It wasn't faith in the absence of evidence, but faith that followed where the evidence led. It was a faith that would be tested in different ways in the years to come.

Due to what Jeremy reckons can only have been an administrative error, he obtained a place at Cambridge when he left his local comprehensive school in Hemel Hempstead. After university he headed for the bright lights of the City and a career in banking. He did a couple of years at Barclays, then at the Bank of Montreal, after which he moved to Credit Suisse where he was to spend the next 21 years – in Switzerland, France, the US, and the UK. He was fast-tracked for senior management, with a year out at INSEAD, the prestigious business school in Paris, and rose quickly through the ranks to become the head of Credit Suisse's UK private banking business. Life as a CEO was demanding, high-pressured, and relentless, especially when things went wrong. As part of a global business you could get a call at 3 a.m. on a Sunday morning and find yourself on a plane to Tokyo the next day to sort out a problem.

But Jeremy found it good fun too, having the power to make decisions and being paid a silly salary. In those boom days of banking, before the financial crisis of 2008, money flowed freely. While entertaining clients he would find himself racing at Goodwood in the bank's classic sports cars, or organising an annual management retreat for a thousand global executives on a cruise liner or at a luxury resort, hiring the likes of John Cleese as the guest speaker.

In 2008 Jeremy was appointed the head of Hoare & Co, the UK's oldest private bank. Founded in 1672, it is owned and led by the Hoare family, whose family home is Stourhead in Wiltshire. Jeremy was the first non-family CEO in the bank's almost 350-year history, and would have lunch every week with the eight family members in the bank's oak-panelled dining room, the walls of which were lined with paintings by Old Masters.

Banking doesn't perhaps have the best reputation, being perceived by many as a greedy, corrupt world of fat cats, and some might question what a committed Christian like Jeremy was doing there. His response is, firstly, that work is a good thing, being part of God's creation pattern for humanity, and God gives people different gifts so they can serve him in a whole range of jobs. He says, 'It's not as if Christians can only serve God as church ministers or missionaries. As long as a job is not immoral or illegal it is an appropriate sphere for the Christian in which they can serve him.' Jeremy was once asked in a job interview if he would lend money to a producer of porn films and said he couldn't because as a Christian he sees that as immoral.

But otherwise he doesn't see any conflict between banking itself and the Christian faith – and they still offered him the job!

Secondly, he explains that banking is a good and necessary part of how society functions, transmitting money from one part of the economy to another, making loans, and so on. Jesus told a parable in which someone is rebuked for not being a good steward of their money with the words, 'you should have put my money on deposit with the bankers, so that when I returned I would have received it back with interest.'[1] Historically Christians have actually been at the forefront of banking. Jeremy points out, 'Barclays bank, to take one example, was an amalgam of various Quaker banks, and until the late 19th century was founded explicitly on Christian values from the Bible.'

Thirdly, he says that the Bible does not condemn money or making money, but the love of money. Sometimes people declare, 'Money is the root of all evil', but it is a misquotation. The verse actually says, 'For the love of money is a root of all kinds of evil.'[2] Money is a good servant, but a bad master. Jeremy quotes the famous saying of Augustine: 'You have made us for yourself, O Lord, and our heart is restless until it rests in you.' He adds, 'It's as if our hearts have a God-shaped hole. Having rejected God, we try to fill the hole with other things – career, money, a relationship. But these false gods cannot satisfy us or save us, and will in the end destroy us.' He has seen plenty of examples of this over the years in the City, where the love of money is a big driver for many. In the first bank where Jeremy worked, back in 1984, a favourite topic of conversation among his colleagues was how much money you needed to make to retire. At that time it was half a million. But the love of money is like drinking salt water. The more you drink, the thirstier you become. Jeremy explains,

> It leaves you like a donkey trying to get the carrot dangling on a stick held out by its rider. You never quite get there and always want more. And it never delivers the happiness it seems to promise. Some of the most miserable people I've met during my career are those consumed by the love of money and who have sacrificed everything – typically marriage and children – on this altar. They are rich and successful, but miserable. And unwilling to acknowledge it, because that would be to admit weakness and to make yourself vulnerable.

He remembers a conversation he had one day about life, the universe and everything with the CEO of a big Swiss bank. The man betrayed no hint of anything amiss, but a week later tragically took his own life. In Jeremy's experience the love of money in the City is not just about the security and toys that money can buy: 'It's actually as much a way of keeping score. A way of measuring yourself against others and feeling successful and having others look up to you. The root is pride and wanting to be in control.'

Jeremy is the first to admit that he has felt the full force of these temptations over the years and has made many mistakes. When he started out in banking he didn't have a good work–life balance and was too driven by money. But being generous in giving away money (as well as time) has been a way of keeping money from becoming his master and getting a hold on him. More generally, in what is often a brutal, backstabbing environment on Wall Street and in the City, he has sought to live out his faith in Christ by behaving in a Christ-like way – seeking to avoid gossip, not saying things about people he wouldn't say to their face, and being honest, truthful and a person of integrity.

Hearing the first 50 years of Jeremy's story, you might be tempted to conclude that Christian faith is a passport to prosperity and happiness, but the past few years give the lie to that and to any notion that being a Christian protects you from the trials of life. Five years ago Jeremy went to the doctor's to get a small lump on his ribs checked out. He was sent from specialist to specialist before finally being referred to The Royal Marsden Hospital that specialises in treating cancer. It turned out he had a stage one cancer and the prognosis was good. He had two operations, then radiotherapy. Six months later he was given the all-clear. Life returned to normal ... until May 2015.

As Jeremy recalls, 'It was a Saturday night. I was round at a friend's house for dinner. I went to adjust the collar on my shirt and felt a large lump the size of a golf ball on my collarbone.' He went back to the Marsden. The following week the results came through. He sat in the waiting room with his wife, Jeanette. When they were called in there were three other specialists with the doctor and a scan picture: 'I'm sorry, Jeremy. The tumours are everywhere. They're incurable. You've got 18 months. We can try and slow it down with chemo, but there's nothing we can do to stop it.'

Jeremy describes how in that space of 30 seconds his life changed forever: 'It's like being in a lift and the floor drops away. It was devastating, and there were many tears.' He was just 53 with a wife and three children. He wanted to live, not die. 'But', he says, 'in it all I also felt a tremendous peace, knowing that my life is in God's hands.' In the months since then his experience has been that cancer can be quite lonely. People are sympathetic, but you know that eventually it will take you away. Yet in it he has felt closer to God than ever before – the God who says in the Bible, 'Never will I leave you; never will I forsake you.'[3]

Jeremy reflects,

Cancer is often boring, involving sitting around for ages. It's humbling. You're not in control. You feel powerless. You face a problem that you can't just throw money at to make it go away. You're suddenly at the bottom of the food chain. You stop working and find yourself in a parallel world of doctors, specialists, and blood tests. Then there's the ordeal every two months of going for a scan, and the anxiety and stress of waiting for the appointment a week later when you get the results. Each one is a mini version of the stomach-churning conversation that marked the beginning of this new life.

For him it has brought into sharp focus that faith is not just about intellectual assent:

> *It's about trust. It's about letting God sit in the driving seat and taking your own hands off the steering wheel. And for people in the City that is one of the hardest things to do. The type of personality who does well in that environment likes to be in charge, to be in control. But there is great peace in knowing that your life is in God's hands and trusting him.*

When Jeremy is tempted to feel 'It's not fair!' or 'Why me?', again he sees it as a question of trust: 'Do I really trust that God is my loving heavenly Father and wants the best for me? It's a bit like being a small child crossing a busy road with his dad. Will I put my hand in his and trust him to take me safely to the other side?' He has found the Bible to be an enormous source of strength and comfort:

> *The Psalms cover the full range of human emotion and experience, and give you words to express what you are feeling to God; the book of Job communicates the perspective that there is a bigger picture we cannot see; and the New Testament, with its teaching that in Christ God suffered for us, reassures us that he therefore knows what we are going through when we are suffering.*

As is often the case in tragedy, comedy is sometimes not far away. To cope with the boredom of radiotherapy and having to lie there perfectly still as the machine does its thing, Jeremy decided to memorise some psalms. On one occasion he chose Psalm 34, which is a psalm of assurance that: 'The LORD is close to the broken-hearted' and 'The angel of the LORD encamps around those who fear him'. But as Jeremy was lying there he suddenly found he couldn't stop chuckling, and ended up being ticked off by the radiotherapist for not keeping still. He'd got up to verse five which says, 'Those who look to him are radiant'!

After his first bout of chemotherapy Jeremy and his wife set off for the holiday of a lifetime in South America. But on the flight out he became aware that the sight in his left eye was deteriorating. A few days later, in a rainforest in Ecuador, everything suddenly went dark. It turned out he had a detached retina, completely unrelated to the cancer. By the time they got back to the UK it was too late to save the eye. A few months later lightning struck twice as the retina in his other eye detached, so for two months he was virtually blind. He says, 'It was terrifying, especially on top of everything else.' Now, some ten operations later, he has reasonable sight in one eye, but comments, 'If you read about hospitals being overwhelmed, I am personally responsible! From never being in hospital, it seems like I am never out of one!'

The biggest challenge is of course that he faces death itself, but in this he is not alone. Jeremy points out,

It is an appointment that none of us can avoid. Death is the 1-in-1 statistic. Everyone will one day be where I am now, facing death. People would rather do anything than think about the reality of death. But it is coming. As Benjamin Franklin supposedly said, "Nothing is certain except death and taxes." Well, some manage to avoid taxes, but we can't avoid death.

For many, death spells futility and despair, but Jeremy believes the best is yet to come: 'Death is going to be with the Lord. When my eyes close in death, I will see him face to face. Preparing for death is like getting ready for a trip to the Seychelles. The destination is wonderful, but Heathrow is a total mess!' He tells the story of a Christian leader from a previous age, Henry Venn, who on his deathbed became so excited when told he was about to see Jesus that he lived for another three months!

Some might dismiss this Christian hope as wishful thinking and escapism, but for Jeremy the issue has always been 'Is it true?' not 'Is it helpful?' He says he knows it is true because of the resurrection of Jesus Christ from the dead. That is the ultimate proof. And in his own experience he testifies to the reality of knowing the Lord is with him and will walk with him through the dark valley of the shadow of death and out the other side into God's eternal kingdom. He states, 'No-one has the cure for cancer, but Jesus has the cure for death. Through him we can have eternal life.'

This is a message he is keen to share with as many as possible, for as long as he has left. He remarks, 'To not do so would be like having the cure for cancer and keeping it to yourself.' The Bible is the world's bestselling book ever, but surprisingly few people have read it, and as a result misconceptions about the Christian faith abound. One of the most common he encounters is the belief that Christians are saying they are better than other people – as if they are at the top of some moral skyscraper, telling others to come and join them on a higher floor. He explains:

> *In fact the message about Jesus is not for good people but for bad people. The Bible says we all fail to live as we should. A Christian is someone who has recognised they are sick and need a doctor, spiritually speaking. It is someone who has accepted the forgiveness Jesus has secured by dying in our place on the cross, rescuing us from the judgement we deserve.*

He is now reading John's Gospel one-to-one with a dozen or so senior executives – former colleagues – who want to find out more. One of his favourite Bible passages is an incident in which Jesus and his disciples are out in a boat when a storm blows up. The boat starts filling with water. The disciples are terrified. Jesus meanwhile is in the stern, fast asleep on a cushion. They wake him up, saying, 'Don't you care?'[4] It's a situation to which Jeremy can relate: 'That is how it can feel at times. It's when the storm is raging, and Jesus doesn't seem to do anything to intervene, that faith is tested. Does he really care? Is he really in control? But I know that he is with me in the boat, and will bring me safely to the other side.'

6

High Court Judge
Jeremy Cooke

Where does the evidence lead?

In 2013 Deutsche Bank faced an $8 billion litigation claim from a Monaco-based investment firm owned by a Norwegian billionaire. The trial in the commercial court lasted four months and involved complex evidence from some 20 factual witnesses and 16 expert witnesses from the US, Switzerland, and various jurisdictions in Asia. There were five counsel on each side, with 'Magic Circle' law firms (that is to say, the top corporate ones) behind them. It took seven weeks for the judge to write his judgement in which he dismissed the claim and ordered the investment firm to pay over $240 million to the bank. The judge at the trial was Mr Justice Cooke.

Weighing up evidence is what Jeremy Cooke does, and has done all his professional life, latterly as a High Court judge. Even a short two-week trial might involve 20 to 25 lever-arch files of material. For a longer trial of three or four months you're looking at 150 to 200 files. A witness statement alone can be 80 to 100 pages long. There's a lot of reading and a lot of listening. That's Jeremy's job – he's trained to evaluate things and make decisions based on the evidence.

In his line of work evidence is what counts. He says, 'Law is based on the premise that truth is discoverable from evidence.' He reminds the jury at the start of a criminal trial, 'Don't investigate on the Internet or look at newspaper reports or talk to your families. Discard everything apart from the evidence you hear in court. Set aside your preconceptions and come to a common-sense conclusion based on the evidence.' Usually the evidence points clearly in one direction or another. In a civil trial you weigh something up on the balance of probabilities. In a criminal trial the jury has to be sure beyond reasonable doubt that the defendant is guilty.

That, Jeremy says, is the approach we also need to adopt to the big questions of life and our search for truth: 'Look at the evidence and evaluate it. Look at the most cogent explanation that best fits the evidence.' This is what he himself has done and this is why he is a Christian today – because of the evidence. Rather than Christian faith flying in the face of the evidence he states, 'Faith is what you believe to be true having followed where the evidence leads – and then acting on it.' And that is the challenge he puts to others:

In 21st-century Britain uncertainty about ultimate issues is the norm. People say, 'I have no faith,' or 'I don't know,' which is a nonsense. Everyone has a worldview, a way of looking at reality. Everyone has beliefs about who we are, what life is about, what is important, and what happens when we die. And we are all living out a worldview. But the question is whether your worldview corresponds to reality. Is it the most cogent conclusion based on the evidence?

This is the sort of rigorous thinking which he finds is often left undone. He asks,

Why does the universe work rationally according to the laws of science? How does humanity with personality and rationality exist if we are just the product of chance? Why is it that we have such capacity for both love and selfishness? Why do we long for meaning if there is none? Where does our sense of justice and right and wrong come from? Why is there religion in every society? A sensible worldview has to take account of all these elements. Your worldview is irrational and illogical if it doesn't.

His own conclusion is:

Christian faith provides the most logically coherent and cogent explanation for those features, and above all for Jesus. The big question to be answered in coming to a worldview turns on Jesus and the evidence he gave on ultimate truth, and the evidence about him. If the

*evidence supports him, then trusting in him is an entirely
rational response and the only logical thing to do.*

From his mid-teens Jeremy was persuaded of the truth
of Christianity. It seemed to him the best explanation of
the world around him and above all of the resurrection
of Jesus, which he saw as the focal point. But although he
believed it was true, for a time he didn't do anything in
response to it. What eventually made the difference was
seeing others, and in particular university students a few
years older than him, whose faith was real and impacted
how they lived. That was the turning point. He says, 'What
came across to me was this: that if Christianity is true, then
it really is what you have to live by. Once I really grasped
that, I realised that what life has to be about is serving God,
being in the place he wants you to be, following Jesus, and
making it real in your own life.'

He got a first class in Law at Oxford, and was a rugby
blue who went on to play for Harlequins. After graduation
he joined a leading firm of City solicitors, and then
became a barrister, becoming Queen's Counsel and rising
to be the head of commercial chambers at 7 King's Bench
Walk. But he spent a long time trying to get out of the
Law. He thought about heading up a missionary society,
or retraining and going off to South America to teach the
Bible. He continues, 'And then it finally dawned on me that
I was actually already in the place where God wanted me
to be. God wanted me out there in the muck of life.' The
rightness of the decision to stay, and the conclusion that

this was the best fit for the particular gifts God had given him, was brought home to him one morning at the age of 52 when he received a call from the Lord Chancellor telling him to come to see him at the House of Lords that afternoon. In those days you didn't apply to become a High Court judge – you were invited. It is in this role that he lived out his Christian faith and served God for the next 15 years.

As a Christian judge his approach to a case would not have been hugely different to a judge who was not Christian. He comments, 'Tragically many judges in the world are corrupt, but in this country at least most of those who become judges have a strong sense of justice. And the law is there to be applied. Getting it right or wrong does not come down to being Christian.' So what difference did it make him being Christian? He answers,

> You hope to come across in a Christ-like way in how you behave and treat other people. As a Christian you have a logical reason for doing justice. You also have a different motivation, wanting to honour and please God. And I would pray for everyone in my court – for the accused, for the lawyers, for the various parties, and that justice would be done. In addition, in my sentencing I would be careful not to condemn the person.

Jeremy has tried many high-profile cases over his career, and a huge variety of them: commercial disputes between multinational companies; cheating in international cricket;

a royal blackmail plot; the stabbing of an MP; a fraudulent bank trader. But in the final analysis they have all come down to one thing, and that is evidence. He explains, 'There is the direct evidence of people who testify, and the hearsay evidence in documents of what people say others have said to them. What lawyers and juries have to do is to look at the evidence, listen to witnesses, assess credibility, and then draw inferences and decide what is true.' The historian, he says, does the same: 'They investigate records, balance different versions of events, and come to a conclusion.' And that, he declares, is what we have to do with the cornerstone of the Christian faith – the resurrection of Jesus Christ.

It's a subject about which Jeremy loves to speak, because this historical event is so foundational and the evidence is so compelling. It also gives him the opportunity to eat daffodils in public! Chomping his way through a couple of daffs is his favourite way to kick off a talk on the resurrection. He advises, 'Only eat the yellow bit, not the stalk, or you'll end up in hospital having your stomach pumped. The yellow bit is actually quite soft, albeit tasteless, and melts in the mouth.' But it's not just an icebreaker; there is a point. He explains,

Imagine going back to your flat and telling your mates that you've just seen a High Court judge eat two daffodils. They might not believe you. But what if 20 or 500 people reported the same, and they were people of integrity? The evidence is what people say they've seen and heard.

You need to evaluate it, look at contrary evidence, and work out what is the most coherent explanation. That is precisely what we have to do with the resurrection of Jesus.

And so he lays out his case. He argues that the gospel records in the Bible are second to none in reliability among ancient manuscripts: 'The originals were all written in the lifetime of eyewitnesses. People who were there at the time record what they say they saw and heard. The copies we have amount to some 25,000 manuscripts of varying antiquity, with the earliest dating back to AD 120. No other writing of antiquity can compare to the Gospels.' The evidence that these accounts put before us is impressive. When Jeremy speaks on the resurrection of Jesus he goes through it methodically, as if summing up the main points for the jury to consider:

Jesus, having been sentenced, flogged, and nailed to a cross through his wrists and heels, had died a long and painful death. Any suggestion that the Roman executioners failed in their job is ridiculous. Jesus was definitely dead. His body had then on that Friday been laid in a rock tomb, ritually washed, and clothed in white linen and spices to allay the smell of decomposition. The tomb was then sealed with a huge millstone weighing some 1.5 tonnes, rolled in place across the entrance, and guarded by a detachment of 16 soldiers. On the Sunday morning the stone was found rolled away, the grave clothes were found lying in the tomb, and the body was gone. And then over a 40-day period lots of people – different characters at different times and in different places – said they had seen Jesus alive. They said they had walked and talked with him, and even touched him.

Jeremy then works through alternative explanations of this evidence and shows how implausible they are, such as the idea that the disciples stole the body. He remarks,

Psychologically it is highly improbable that a group like this, who as followers of Jesus accorded truth and integrity the highest value, would make up such a story out of the depths of terror and disappointment they felt when Jesus was killed, and then within weeks be persuading thousands of others. And it would require all 16 guards falling asleep; the disciples sneaking past them; rolling away the huge stone without making a noise; unwrapping the body from the sticky grave clothes; carrying it out past the guards into the night; and then spreading a story about the resurrection which they knew to be false but for which they were prepared to die. How likely is that?

He goes on to argue as well for the impossibility of the idea that those who say they saw Jesus after his death suffered from mass hallucination. He sums up with a challenge: 'You can't dismiss the accounts because of preconceptions that dead men don't rise, or that there is nothing beyond the material, or that they were just fabricated. Examine the evidence and don't close your mind. Start from the empty tomb. Many have been persuaded, including two Lord Chief Justices and one Lord Chancellor.'

Some might think it all much ado about nothing, but the significance of the resurrection of Jesus cannot be overstated. He explains, 'Jesus claimed to be God himself on earth. The resurrection vindicated that claim. If it happened then Jesus is who he says he is, and that has cosmic and personal significance. All of us then need to do something about it.' It also means that death is not the end and one day we will all meet God as Judge.

The very idea of someone sitting in judgement, whether in a human or divine court, is not always a popular one, as Jeremy has found from personal experience. He has the dubious honour of having been burned in effigy not just once but twice. The first time was in Lewes in East Sussex. Two men who ran a fireworks business had been illegally storing military-grade explosives in a storage container among their legitimate fireworks. The container caught fire, the fire brigade were called, and then the whole thing exploded, killing two of the firemen. As the judge at the trial he sent down the two owners for manslaughter. It so happened that the two convicted men were patrons of one of Lewes' ten bonfire societies who get together annually on 5 November to build and burn a large effigy of someone unpopular. Jeremy found himself the target that year.

The second occasion was in Karachi. In 2011 three of Pakistan's international cricketers were jailed for deliberately bowling no-balls in the previous year's

Test Match against England as part of a spot-fixing betting scam. Although the guilt of the young men was indisputable, not all the cricket fans back in the home country were best pleased to see their stars sent to prison. And so Jeremy, having been the judge in that case too, met his fate again.

At another trial, this time of an Islamic extremist who stabbed MP Stephen Timms, there were shouts of 'curse the judge' from the public gallery as he sentenced the woman responsible. Jeremy accepts that such hostility comes with the territory: 'You're making decisions with serious repercussions – life in prison, for example. It's not going to make you popular with their families and friends. But I'm doing what God has put me in this place to do. I try to serve him and do my job to the best of my abilities.'

If human judges are at times unpopular, how much more so God as Judge. Many people have little time for the idea of God judging everyone at the end of history, but Jeremy sees things quite differently: 'Judgement is about putting things right. It's blindingly obvious to anyone that this world needs putting right, and so it is very positive that God will in the end put it right. In fact it is impossible that a good God wouldn't do that.' And whereas human courts make mistakes, God won't. Jeremy continues, 'Human justice is rough and ready. We have to judge from what people do and say, and draw conclusions about what they intended to do. We can get it wrong. But God gets it right all the time, 100%. He can see what is going on inside people. That is a great comfort.' It is however fairly uncomfortable as well, knowing that one day we will all be on the receiving end of such perfect, all-knowing justice, as Jeremy is the first to admit. He in no way sees himself on the moral high ground as a judge – as he made clear to the Queen when they were having a chat one day!

One of the perks of becoming a High Court judge is that a knighthood comes as part of the package. And so off he trotted to Buckingham Palace to meet the Queen and have her do her thing with a sword. You spend ten minutes with her before she rings a little bell to signal your time is up, but the etiquette is that she must begin the conversation. Her Majesty asked him about criminals and whether he thought they were different to other people. It was a subject in which she had some personal interest, having recently had an unnerving stand-off for three-quarters of an hour with an intruder she found at the bottom of her bed. Jeremy's response was that criminals are not really different at all to the rest of us. They face the same temptations we all do, only in their case they may feel them more strongly because of their circumstances. He said, 'We're all in the same boat.'

This conviction actually shapes the way he sentences people: 'Some judges might say in sentencing, "You are a very wicked person." I would say, "What you have done is very wicked. And you need to face the consequences for that." I'm not pointing the finger and saying they are completely different from me, but rather that they have done something wrong that requires they be punished.'

The High Court judge is all too aware that he himself will one day stand before the ultimate Judge, and it is a sobering prospect. He explains,

The reality is that many serious crimes I've dealt with are committed by people whose circumstances are so different to mine, but I'm always conscious that their problems are at root exactly the same as my problems – living for self, and not putting God at the centre. I would be ashamed and fearful of having all my life exposed, with all its petty selfishness, and open before God. Not many of us would be happy for our nearest and dearest to see any of it. That is why I am enormously grateful that I am in Christ, and so have nothing to fear.

It is here that we are brought to the heart of the Christian message. God as Judge has done something quite inconceivable for a human judge. He has taken on himself the judgement we deserve. Jeremy says he did once hear of a magistrate paying a £50 victim surcharge on behalf of a defendant who couldn't afford it and who otherwise faced going to prison. Yet such an instance is highly unusual and the magistrate was reprimanded for it. 'But', he continues, 'the wonder of the Christian gospel is that God, in the person of Christ, has taken on himself all the consequences of our evil and paid for it. It is mysterious and astonishing. The grace of it is overwhelming.'

However if the message is such good news and the evidence so compelling, why don't more people accept it? Why are there not more Christian judges? Jeremy is not surprised. He responds, 'The intellectual stuff only takes you so far. In the end it is a question of the will. I've known people who have accepted intellectually that it is true, but have then said that it's not for them.' It may seem astonishing, given what is at stake, but it is sadly all too common. The problem in the end, he says, is not with the evidence: 'The issue is whether or not we are prepared to follow where the evidence leads and to act on it.'

7

Bake Off Star
Martha Collison

Why bother with God when you're young?

A few years ago no-one had heard of Martha Collison. She was just a Berkshire schoolgirl, hanging out with friends, getting on with her homework, and working part-time on the cheese counter in her local Waitrose. Then overnight she was catapulted into a celebrity world in which she found people staring at her in Nando's and stopping her in the street. People wanted her autograph and would take selfies with her. People she'd never met would send her cards and gifts. You'd be forgiven for thinking she was part of the latest chart-topping girl band, but in her case the reason for all the attention was not music but food.

Martha is seriously into food. It's her passion. She loves cooking and loves baking. By her mid-teens she was cooking for her family every evening and baking every weekend, and had her heart set on studying food science at university. She says, 'I was a real cookery geek. I wasn't just interested in how to make things but the chemistry behind the recipe. Why does bread rise? Why does slow-cooking lamb make it so delicious?' Then one day, really just for fun and any excuse for putting off homework, she sent in an application for the TV show *The Great British Bake Off*. She didn't think she would hear anything more of it, never mind be invited for an audition. As for getting on the show, never in a million years would that happen. There were typically as many as 35,000 applicants for the 12 places.

But a few months later she was sitting outside the iconic tent with legendary food writer and *Bake Off* judge Mary Berry, eating ice lollies on a hot summer's afternoon. At just 17 she had become the youngest ever contestant on the show. She won the hearts of the nation and went all the way to the quarter-finals. Now, three years on, she is the author of two cookbooks, has her own weekly column with Waitrose alongside the likes of Pippa Middleton and Mariella Frostrup, and travels the country giving talks and cookery demonstrations. She comments, 'I do things every day that girls my age don't do, and it's just so exciting. *Bake Off* has completely turned my life upside down.' So much in her life has changed, but what has kept her stable and grounded is the core that has remained the same – her family, her friends, and her Christian faith.

Having grown up in a Christian home, coming to a personal faith in Christ was nothing dramatic, but is no less strong or real for that. She explains, 'For me it all comes down to the person of Jesus. I believe he is the Son of God who died and rose again. My whole faith is built on this. I'm forgiven and God's grace is for me.' Sometimes the assumption from the outside can be that church is dull and only for the elderly, but Martha's experience since a young age in a vibrant, all-age congregation in Ascot says otherwise. She continues, 'I love my church. It's full of family and friends and fun, and I love being part of it'. She made a personal commitment to Christ at the age of eight. Her Christian faith now is heartfelt, thought-through, lived-out, and focused.

In February 2015 she was on stage in Birmingham Cathedral alongside Archbishop Justin Welby, teaching him how to bake sticky toffee pudding in front of 300 young people at an event called 'Recipe for Life' – just one of the many, varied, and sometimes unusual spin-offs of her new life as a *Bake Off* star. She talked him through what to do, while he quizzed her in front of everyone. He asked her what the difference was between believing in God and being a Christian disciple. She replied, 'Knowing that Jesus is alive. He died for me, rose again, and is living and moving in this generation.' He asked her how that works out day to day. Does she spend all day praying, or if not what difference does it make? She explained, 'God lives in me by his Holy Spirit, as he does in all who follow Jesus. In everything I do I try to be God focused. God is at the heart of my life.' That was just as true during the *Bake Off* experience as at other times. Martha says, 'My faith is very important to me and did help me get through difficult times. It helped me keep going when I felt I was crumbling.'

Perhaps talk of 'difficult times' and 'crumbling' sounds melodramatic for a cookery programme, but that would be to underestimate the pressures of featuring in a show like this. *The Great British Bake Off* is a very big deal in the UK. The 12 home bakers take part in a televised 'bake-off' which tests every aspect of their baking skills, as they battle it out to stay on the show and be crowned the best amateur baker. Over the course of 10 weeks of intense competition, set in a marquee in the grounds of a country estate, renowned British bakers (at that time, Mary Berry and Paul Hollywood) judge the contestants on their skills at making cakes, pastries, breads, and desserts. The popularity of the show has grown every year since its launch on the BBC in 2010, such that it is now an established part of British culture. In 2014, the year Martha competed, more people watched the *Bake Off* final than the World Cup football final – 12.1 million tuned in to see Germany beat Argentina in Brazil, but 12.3 million viewers were glued to their screens to see who would be crowned *Bake Off* champ. When one particular contestant was evicted in last year's programme, a newspaper declared it 'a national day of mourning'.

It is quite some spotlight to be under, not least as a 17-year-old, when the next youngest contestant is 31, and when you're putting in 16-hour days in the *Bake Off* tent while revising for the AS level exams you're sitting during the week. Martha explains, 'We'd go to our bakers' room over lunchbreak, and I'd bring out my chemistry text books. The other bakers would look at me like I'm crazy.'

On top of that, the fact that you're on the show has to be kept secret from all but immediate family and a few close friends until it airs. Then, to cap it all, you have to cope with Paul Hollywood giving your cake the long stare. Martha remarks, 'That is definitely the most intimidating part. He does the stare, and then he'll either go, "That's the best thing I've ever tasted," or, "That's disgusting," And you just don't know which way he'll go.'

Her Christian faith certainly helped her cope with the pressure. She observes, 'My faith gives me a sense of perspective. I am well aware there are more important things in life than baking the perfect ciabatta.' But, even so, it was emotionally draining and took its toll. At one point she almost fainted from exhaustion with the heat and stress, and was reduced to tears when Mary Berry gave a withering assessment of her custard tart's 'soggy bottom'. The wheels really came off in week seven, when her experimental maple syrup and bacon eclairs went pear-shaped. She says, 'I was juggling revising with baking, and it was just a bit of a car-crash moment. You're overcome with emotion because you're so tired and you've worked so hard for that one thing.'

But the *Bake Off* experience as a whole was amazing and seems to have set her up for life. As soon as the show finished, she was linked up with an agent and wrote her first book, *Twist: Creative Ideas to Reinvent Your Baking*.[1] Her second book, *Crave: Brilliantly Indulgent Recipes*,[2] has just been published. She even got to bake for the Queen's 90th birthday celebration in Windsor. Martha, along with 2015

Bake Off winner Nadiya Hussain, was asked to provide the cakes, and also met the Queen and Prince Philip. She describes, 'It was a huge honour and I had to pinch myself to make sure I wasn't dreaming.' Not many teenagers get opportunities like that.

But being a young celebrity comes at a price:

Social media is massive for young people. Not everyone likes you, and that's hard to deal with when you're young. I'd type my name into Twitter and get 20,000 hits, one in 20 of which would be negative. I would be personally attacked on every level – for the way I dressed, my hair, my looks, my upbringing – and some of it was pretty vile.

She had never before been the object of such hatred and venom, but says, 'How I look or what others think of me is not where I take my worth. It's not what defines me. God made me as I am, and I am loved in Christ. And God doesn't focus on the outward appearance but on the heart.'

The social media abuse aside, Martha is very aware of how privileged she is, and is keen to use her newfound fame and baking skills to help those less fortunate than herself – which is how she found herself in Cambodia, a country whose people have suffered enormously. A couple of things struck her on arrival. Firstly, that there were lots of young people and old people, but very few in between. There was a missing generation, wiped out in the 'killing fields' of the '70s and '80s. Secondly, the extreme poverty:

'People with no shoes, no food, no jobs, and drinking out of a dirty lake. It made me more passionate about using what I've got to help others.'

But the specific reason she was there was the epidemic of sex trafficking, a poisonous weed growing in the soil of poverty. The statistics speak for themselves – one child is trafficked every 30 seconds. Martha met a girl called Shrinang who lives alone with her mother. She's the youngest of five siblings. The older four were all sold and taken to Thailand, and haven't been seen since. She has no idea what happened to them, but fears the worst. It's a desperate but well-trodden path. Battling extreme rural poverty at home, with large families which parents can't support, then the promise of a better life for their children in the foreign city, yet little understanding because of the language barrier, and getting trapped in debt because of poor pay. One in three children are exploited and abused in the sex trade. How baking could make a difference might not seem immediately obvious, but that is why Martha was in Cambodia.

The Christian charity Tearfund, whose strapline is 'Following Jesus where the need is greatest', runs practical workshops as part of their 'No Child Taken' campaign. The purpose is to train people and give them a skill – such as agriculture, motorbike repair, sewing, or baking – which they can use to start a small business and earn money, therefore making them less vulnerable to the lure of the traffickers. It was at one of these workshops that Martha came across Shrinang. Thanks to the skills this

12-year-old girl is learning, she is now no longer afraid of the future and is able to support her mother. Martha, who has become an ambassador for Tearfund, says, 'Everything I'm good at is because God has gifted me at it and is for his glory. I want to use it to make a difference and to show the love of Jesus. God can heal broken lives.'

The same motivation led to her getting involved on her return to the UK with a new Christian charity called Bramber Bakehouse, which uses baking to give confidence and hope to women rescued from trafficking in this country. Martha is one of a small team of part-time workers running a monthly Saturday morning baking workshop. The difference it is making to the women who attend inspires their dream of turning it one day into a full-time bakery.

It's been an extraordinary journey for Martha over the past few years. Where this path will lead in the future she doesn't know, but is happy for now to just keep enjoying the adventure, walking with God one bake at a time. For her the beauty of baking and cooking is that it brings together two of her passions – food and people. She comments, 'Food is not just fuel, but an amazing way of connecting with people. I like to share what I make with other people, and turn what is an essential part of life, namely eating, into a joyful experience. Meals are about enjoying friendship and fellowship together as you sit down around a table with them.'

The Bible pictures the eternal kingdom of God as a wonderful banquet to which we are all invited, paid for by the death of Jesus – but whether we will get to be there depends on how we respond to God's invitation. In one story Jesus told, those invited to the feast just made excuses – they were too busy with other things, or not interested – and ended up shut out of the party.[3] But to those who accept the invitation, the reality of a relationship with God in eternity begins even now in this life. In the final book of the Bible Jesus says, 'I stand at the door and knock. If anyone hears my voice and opens the door, I will come in and eat with that person, and they with me.'[4] That is a meal deal not to miss out on!

8

Metals Trader
Michael Farmer

Is Jesus still alive?

My sister and I were born at the end of the war, and both our parents were alcoholics. Our father died from this when I was four, and violence was a part of that backdrop. We were soon bankrupt and, with a mother still struggling with drink, we experienced the poverty, neglect, and shame that are such potent drivers of social exclusion.

Given such a start in life, no-one could have imagined, least of all Michael Farmer himself, that one day he would be giving this account of his troubled childhood in the grand setting of the Lords Chamber in the Palace of Westminster as a member of the House of Lords. This self-made multi-millionaire had earned the nickname 'Mr Copper' while making his fortune in the international metal markets. But what defines him as a person is not his rags-to-riches story, nor the success and influence he has enjoyed, but a close encounter he had as he lay in bed one night at the age of 35. His life would never be the same again.

His memories of his early years are not happy ones. He was sent off to boarding school at the age of six and had a rough time. He struggled in class. He was bullied by other pupils, and remembers being beaten with a walking stick by the headmaster in front of the whole school for eating a crab apple during a lesson. The only good thing about boarding school was the escape from his home environment, but he was forever worrying about what was happening with his sister and alcoholic mother.

When he left school the metals trading company of which his late father had been the director gave Michael a job out of a sense of loyalty. He started on the very lowest rung of the ladder, earning £8 a week as a 'difference account clerk'. It was at a subsequent company that he learned his trade in metals. He explains that unlike brokerage, where you fulfil orders on behalf of others, this was physical trading in which you are the principal, buying copper in, say, Zambia and shipping it to China. He went on to work at Philipp Brothers, who dominated the physical metal markets in the 1970s. It was here that Michael became a protégé of the brilliant and inspirational Manfred Kopelman and under him learned the ropes in the ring of the London Metal Exchange.

It was an education for which he is very thankful, but it was a steep learning curve and not for the faint-hearted. Manfred was a genius who didn't suffer fools gladly.

Michael says,

On one occasion he told me to sell a thousand tonnes to a broker on the other side of the ring, but I got the wrong chap. This earned me a sharp cuff round the head and a, 'Not him, you idiot.' After another trade that went wrong he stopped talking to me for months. I was pretty stunned, but I had a choice: either pack it in or work out how to do it better.

Back in the open-plan office, shouting between colleagues seemed to be the order of the day. It took a while for Michael to get used to the culture, but after engaging in a good high-decibel exchange one day about diverting some copper to Japan that was due to be shipped from Rotterdam to Shanghai, he finally heard the words, 'Now you're getting it'. It was then that it clicked that it was all about making money. It was something at which Michael was to become very good.

Later on in the 1990s he went on to run MG Metals for 10 years, turning it into the world's biggest copper trader. At its height they were responsible for shipping 15% of Chinese copper imports. It became the first metals trading company to list on the London Stock Exchange, and within 10 months of the float he had received a takeover bid. He recalls, 'The bid was 60% higher than the float price and was in cash.' The buyer was the American energy giant, Enron. Little did Michael know that a year later it, one of America's largest corporations, would collapse almost overnight in a scandal that would shake Wall Street to its core.

After helping the auditors untangle this mess, it was a question of what next for Michael. Retire at 58? He took a two-year break doing something completely different, then decided to set up a hedge fund with a former colleague. RK Capital Management, whose main fund is Red Kite, started with $25 million, which for a hedge fund is small. It's a risky business and finding investors was hard. Having poured in their own money, they started trading in January 2005. At the time the copper price was just $3000 a tonne, but the market took off and by the following year the price had soared to $8900. The hedge fund suddenly found itself sitting on $2.5 billion worth of funds.

You get a flavour of how things are going now, over a decade later, in this excerpt from an article in *The Times* in 2014:

Information at the London Metal Exchange, the world's largest exchange for metals and whose prices are used as benchmarks in contracts around the world, showed that on Tuesday and Wednesday last week a single owner held between 80 and 90 per cent of the copper in stock in its system.

Red Kite Group, a hedge fund led by Michael Farmer, has been identified by brokers and traders as the dominant holder of copper, according to The Wall Street Journal.[1]

But it hasn't all been plain sailing. Success can attract unwelcome attention from predators. After one particularly good year they found themselves attacked by two or three New York hedge funds working together to target them. The intention was to move the market against Red Kite to force losses, and it worked spectacularly well. Within 12 days they were down 30%, having made massive losses. It damaged their reputation and undermined investor confidence in them for years to come. The stress was enormous and Michael was sleeping for just an hour a night. He comments, 'It was like having your arm cut off.' But it was his Christian faith that helped him through and gave him perspective.

God had not featured at all in his home life as a child. At school he had endured chapel, morning and evening, but says, 'It was just English folk religion. There was no relationship with God.' An aunt who was a missionary in Nepal and India, working in a leper colony, had given him a leather-bound Bible which he never read. Inside the front cover she had written a verse from the Psalms: 'Open my eyes, that I may behold wonderful things from your law.'² He had no idea what it meant, but it intrigued him. The same aunt arranged for him to go on a couple of Scripture Union Christian summer camps, but he saw this just as an opportunity for more delinquent behaviour.

Shortly after getting married he moved out to the countryside in Buckinghamshire. He and his wife, Jenny, hardly knew anyone and kept to themselves. Michael's mantra was the Simon & Garfunkel lyric: 'I am a rock. I am an island.' His experience had told him that people hurt you, so don't allow them to get close. But for the first time he found himself wondering if there was more to life. One catalyst was his wife becoming pregnant with their first child. He found it raised all sorts of questions in his mind: 'Who or what is this person coming into the world? And why? And how could a new human being that is so complex and extraordinary be just the product of chance?' There were questions he couldn't help but ask about the natural world as well. He adds, 'We lived out in the fields. I would cut the grass a lot, and would be aware of the seasons and the crops growing and apples trees producing fruit, and then the stars at night. It all seemed so amazing and complex, how it all works.'

Then there was an odd incident when his wife asked her doctor how she could help a woman she knew whose husband was having an affair. The doctor told Jenny to encourage her friend to mix with people who go to church. It seemed a strange thing to say. When Michael heard about this on his return from work that day, his response was: 'You must be kidding.' But then on reflection he thought that maybe the doctor was on to something. At least such people would be kind and try to help. And then one winter's evening the local church minister knocked on the door. Although he never mentioned God once over the cup of tea that followed, it still made an impression on Michael: 'No-one else had done that in five years of us being there.'

At this time, therefore, there were some stirrings in his mind and heart about whether there might be more to life, but that was it – until one night in November 1979. Michael describes,

I had gone to bed as usual and fallen asleep. I don't know what time it was, but at some point in the night I woke up to hear a voice. The voice said a single word: 'Michael'. I wasn't scared, but found myself replying, 'Yes, Lord?' I then saw a bright light in front of my eyes and the words, as if written there, 'Jesus Christ is the Son of God'. It struck me that this changes everything – the whole meaning of my life; who I am; what I'm doing here; my understanding of everything.

It also struck Michael that he knew nothing about God and needed to learn by starting to read the Bible and go to church. His next thought about church, as he lay there in bed, was, 'Don't let them make you treasurer! You need to learn.'

And so, as he went down to breakfast the following morning, a new life began. He says, 'It was pretty scary for my wife, Jenny. She had gone to bed with Michael her husband and had woken up with a Christian. What would it mean? Would they have to go off somewhere as missionaries?' Initially she was very sceptical and resistant. But over time she listened to recordings of Bible talks; met Christians; discovered they were normal people; asked questions; found out more; and came to a personal faith in Christ. There was no sudden conversion in her case, like the apostle Paul's 'Damascus Road' experience.³ Faith for her came as a result of a more gradual and less dramatic process over time, but it was no less strong or real for that. A couple of months after Michael's night-time encounter he was sitting in a sandwich bar on Bishopsgate in the City and noticed a guy he recognised but couldn't place. The man came in again the next day and this time introduced himself. It turned out Michael had seen him at the same little local church out where he lived. He continues,

> He told me there was a church round the corner in the City that teaches the Bible at lunchtime for half an hour. It was just what I needed. I started going and lapped it up. The Bible was explained in a clear way that connected with real life. They taught about who Jesus is and what he had done through his death for our sins on the cross.

As Michael's faith and understanding grew, so did his awareness of his own rebelliousness against God. 'But,' he says, 'I knew that I am forgiven and loved because of Christ, and that he is changing me.'

This change in him was apparent to everyone. One of his first prayers had been, 'Lord, please don't let anyone know I'm a Christian!' But within two years everyone at the Metal Exchange knew. Michael doesn't force his faith on anyone, but just prays, 'Lord, raise up seeking people who want to know more about you.' And God has. Over the decades since many colleagues have come with Michael to listen to those lunchtime Bible talks. One of them is a man who had himself come to faith in Christ – the same man with whom Michael would later set up the hedge fund. They would invite colleagues and business friends along, and together they became known as 'the God squad', but it didn't faze them. At Michael's 40th birthday party the chairman of the London Metal Exchange summed up in a speech he gave in his house what everyone could see. He simply said, 'Michael is not the same as he was.'

Although still hugely successful, coming to know Jesus Christ changed Michael's outlook on work. When at Philipp Brothers, he was asked to join the top trade committee in the world by the chairman in New York. It was a great honour, but he felt he needed to come clean before accepting it. Having prayed about the decision, he replied, 'I'm happy to do it, but you need to know one thing about me – I'm a Christian. So God is the most important thing in my life, then my family, and then work. In that order. I won't be sacrificing my wife and children on the altar of work.'

Michael's faith in Christ shapes everything about his working life – the way he relates to colleagues, the way he makes decisions, and how he deals with stress. At the time of the attack by the New York hedge funds, when he was having sleepless nights, he prayed a lot and asked others to pray. But a turning point in his perspective on the situation came when his church minister said to him, 'You know, God is sovereign. He knows what is happening and is allowing it to happen.' And Michael thought, 'Of course. My heavenly Father is in charge and at work. I just need to trust him.' It helped him relax and carry on, just doing the best he could.

With hindsight Michael can also see the good that has come from this difficult time. In one verse in the Bible God warns his people, 'You may say to yourself, "My power and the strength of my hands have produced this wealth for me." But remember the LORD your God, for it is he who gives you the ability to produce wealth.'⁴ Michael puts it this way:

> *Having done so well there was a real temptation to feel chuffed with myself and think I was such a good guy. But through this experience I was humbled. And though painful that was a good thing, because it forced me to cling to God and depend on him. The Bible says that to keep us from becoming proud, God works in power through our weakness.*

Whereas the first half of Michael's life had been driven by money and career, in the second half of his life a different purpose took over. He explains it as: 'To grow in love for God and to allow him to work through me. To grow in knowledge and love of God the Father, his Son Jesus Christ, my Saviour, and the Holy Spirit. I also pray every morning, "Lord, give me work to do for you today and make my heart glad in doing it."' Part of this work is putting to good use the wealth God has entrusted to him. He has always sought to keep to the biblical principle of giving freely so that your right hand shouldn't even know what your left hand is doing,[5] never mind other people. Generous giving is not for show and praise, but for God's eyes only, and Michael has done that in giving generously but secretly to countless causes. Yet when it comes to political donations, that information is in the public domain. Michael features high up on the list of Britain's biggest political donors.

He is clear about his reasons: 'I'm not giving away my hard-earned money for fun. I'm giving it because I want to fund something I genuinely believe in. The core unit of society – husband, wife, parents, children – has been dismantled. Some people's idea of a family is three people who share a fridge.' He met with David Cameron in 2006 to share his concerns and they spoke about the importance of the family. In 2010 Cameron pledged to make the family a focus of the Tory campaign. Whether or not you agree with Michael's political colours, his concerns are understandable given his upbringing. He continues,

Politicians from happy families are often not that bothered about the breakdown of the family, but those who haven't been so fortunate recognise the value of it. I remember the best man at my wedding, a wonderful Jewish friend, taking me to his home in Surrey. He introduced me to his mother and father. There was family and love. And I left thinking what a good thing it was, and that I'd had no experience of it.

Michael is passionate not just about the family but about wider issues of social justice, and is a dedicated supporter of the Centre for Social Justice. It is no surprise that his maiden speech at the House of Lords was in a debate on women facing homelessness, domestic violence, and social exclusion. These are issues about which he feels very deeply because of his and his sister's painful first-hand experience of them.

Now aged 72 he jokes that he's at the stage of life where bits of him are starting to fall off – in fact he suffers from rheumatoid arthritis – but getting older and facing death are not things he fears. He says, 'I actually find getting older exciting. Every day is one day nearer meeting the Lord. The reality of eternity is huge: being with our Creator and his people for ever, with eternal bodies, with no more suffering or struggle or decay or death.' This certain hope he has about life beyond the grave is because of Jesus:

Jesus taught about the broad road that leads to destruction and the narrow path that leads to life. Jesus is that narrow way. It's as if we live under a massively thick brass dome with no way out. From dust we come and to dust we return. But in that brass ceiling is a little cross-shaped doorway that opens through into eternal life. The Bible says, 'God so loved the world that he gave his one and only Son, that whoever believes in him shall not perish but have eternal life.'[6]

The encounter he had in the middle of the night all those years ago was a one-off experience – for now at least. Michael adds, 'One day I will die. As I lose consciousness here, my next conscious moment will be in front of Jesus Christ. And I will hear that voice say again, "Michael". And I will say, "Oh Lord, you did it."'

9

Major General
Tim Cross

What is life's biggest decision?

'Leadership is about listening, making a decision and getting on with it,' says Tim Cross. These are matters about which he speaks with some authority, having commanded at every level in the British Army, from leading a small bomb disposal team in Northern Ireland in the 1970s to commanding a division of 30,000. Over the course of a 43-year-long distinguished career he has had to make some big decisions. One is the moment he was standing in a field in the Balkans on the Macedonian border when his mobile rang. 'If I let these people in, can you guarantee you will look after them?' the voice asked. On the other end was the Macedonian Foreign Minister, later to become President. The people in question were tens of thousands of refugees waiting on the border. Their fate, and indeed their lives, depended on the decision Tim would make and the answer he would give. But in his view the biggest decision he ever made was on his 30th birthday, standing not in a field but in a garden in Jerusalem. He says, 'I was a young captain at the time, and my life would never be the same again.' It was a decision that was to change not just his life, but the lives of those thousands of refugees all those years later.

Tim's father had worked for Shell, and as result the family had moved around the world following his job, but for Tim the Army was all he had ever wanted. From being an Army cadet he progressed to Sandhurst and was commissioned into the Army in 1971. After a year in Germany and a three-year in-service degree he had his first posting in Northern Ireland. It was a brutal introduction to a brutal world.

Northern Ireland in the mid-70s was in the grip of the so-called 'Troubles', and as head of the ammunitions inspectorate Tim was kept busy. He was part of the specialist 321 EOD (Explosive Ordnance Disposal) unit, which had been deployed to tackle increased violence and the use of bombs by the Provisional IRA (Irish Republican Army). The unit's call sign was 'Felix' – from the idea that a cat has nine lives! Whenever a terrorist device was uncovered, the call would come to 'Fetch Felix'. Tim's first call-out was to a restaurant where the IRA had planted a bomb consisting of a can of petrol, explosives, and a bag of washing powder flakes. The idea was that when it went off the powder flakes would be set alight and become very sticky. The wave of fire would then sweep napalm-like through the crowded room of diners, sticking to them. It was crude but effective, as Tim was to witness first-hand. His unit arrived after the bomb had detonated.

The IRA's regular idea of fun on a Friday night would be to hijack a dozen cars, put a bomb in one of them, and park them in different locations around Belfast. The city would then come to a standstill as the unit responded to a coded warning and tried to locate and deal with the device before it detonated. For 'Felix' it was a deadly game of cat and mouse with a brutal bunch of terrorists. There were shootings, kidnappings, and kneecappings, and at its peak the death toll from the conflict was almost 300 a year.

In the early 80s though Tim ended up in the much less brutal and altogether more pleasant setting of the island of Cyprus in the Mediterranean on a tour with the United Nations, running a detachment in Nicosia. As the UN had deployments all over the Middle East, UN planes would regularly fly between countries to deliver personnel and documentation, and if there was space you could hitch a ride. And so one Easter weekend Tim and his wife found spare seats on a flight to Jerusalem and hopped aboard to enjoy a minibreak.

On Easter Sunday they joined the throngs of tourists at the Church of the Holy Sepulchre, which is supposedly at the site where Jesus was crucified and buried. After a short service they went for a coffee to get away from the crowds, and it was there that someone asked them if they had been to the Garden Tomb. They had never even heard of it. In those days it was underdeveloped and peaceful, not yet being on the main tourist route, so it was a welcome retreat.

An ex-British Army colonel by the name of Dobbie was working there as a guide and showed them round. At the end of the tour, having read some passages from the Bible, he took Tim to one side, looked him in the eye, and spoke to him man to man, in the kind of straight-talking way that military men like. He told him,

Look, all of this is interesting; quite important in some respects. But actually the key issue is this: you go and look in that tomb. It's empty. Now this may or may not have been the exact place Jesus' body was buried – it fits and I think it is – but the important thing is that on that first Easter Sunday morning the tomb was empty. That's the decisive point in history. If you accept that, you cannot allow your life to stay the same. And if you don't accept it, you need to understand the consequences of it.

Tim recalls, 'Feeling a little foolish, I walked across the garden to look inside this first-century tomb which, not surprisingly, was empty. But as I stood at the door of the tomb and looked in, I thought, "He's right. This is important. If this is true, it is a momentous event. A unique event."' It proved to be a turning point in his life.

It's not as if he had never heard anything about such things before. He was not from a churchgoing family, but he has memories of being sent to church on his own as a small boy, and sitting through cold, dark, miserable services in old English. He was confirmed when he was at Sandhurst. Then he and his wife were married in the local church, had their three children baptised there, and went along to a fair number of services as they moved around the world. Tim had heard about Christ being 'the light of the world' and 'the Lamb of God, who takes away the sin of the world,'[1] but had never given much thought to any of it or explored it. He explains,

I'd heard all these expressions, but what did they mean? If they were connected at all with this empty tomb, I needed to explore that and understand it. If this tomb was empty, it's a hugely important issue. I couldn't ignore this any longer and pretend it's nice but makes no difference to me. And if the purpose of Christ's coming was somehow to take away the rottenness of a brutal world, I needed to look into it. I might in the end reject it, but drifting along aimlessly, trying to be a nice bloke, wasn't going to cut it for me.

Back in Cyprus over the following two months he read the bible and studied it for himself. He talked to people he knew and respected and asked and discussed questions. He made the most of the space to think while out and about in the countryside with his detachment. But it was not just an intellectual exercise. He adds,

As a military officer I thought, 'I need to make a decision. I can't sit on the fence or play around with this. I'm either in or out.' And so I made the decision to become a disciple of Christ. I decided this was it and I would pick up the pieces and move forward, accepting the consequences of following Christ whatever the cost. There was no

overwhelming experience or blinding flash, but I felt at
peace and that it was the right thing to have done.

A good friend of his, a senior officer with whom he served later in the First Gulf War, subsequently explained it to him like this: 'Most people who become Christians do so by driving down the M1 or the M2. The M1 is Paul's blinding experience in which Jesus appeared to him on the road to Damascus (one "m"). The M2 is the risen Jesus teaching the Scriptures to the two disciples on the road to Emmaus (two "m"s).'² Tim comments, 'I'm more of an M2 man than M1. I'm a head-driven bloke.'

Having made his decision, two men in particular were to have a significant influence on Tim in his early years as a Christian, learning what it means to follow Christ. The first was the minister of the English-speaking church near Versailles, at the time Tim was posted to Paris on the MILAN anti-tank guided weapons programme. Tim's initial attraction to Christ had been partly at the level of Christ as a man: 'As I looked in the tomb and studied the Bible, Christ was a person I found admirable. He was physically and morally courageous. Someone with a strong sense of identity and purpose. Someone who was clear what life was about and what he wanted to achieve. That appealed to me as a military guy. It was very attractive.' But it was during his time in Paris that his understanding of who Jesus is and what he had come to achieve grew and deepened: 'I came to see that Christ had died for me. Grace, God's undeserved love and forgiveness through Christ, became really important to me. I realised that grace was for me, and I needed it, as well as it being available for anyone else.'

It changed how he related to God:

Before, God was distant. There was no personal relationship. Now, I knew God as my heavenly Father who loves me. I wouldn't have thought that way before, but now I knew it and was very comfortable saying it. He had adopted me into his family and loved me unconditionally, so I didn't need to prove myself. That meant a lot to me as someone who had been adopted as a child.

The second man of influence was a Padre who had been in the Falklands Islands with the Parachute Regiment and whom Tim got to know when he was posted to Germany. The first sermon he heard him give made a big impression. It was from Revelation chapter 3, in which Jesus tells the half-hearted church in Laodicea that he is going to spit them out of his mouth unless they change their ways. The title of the sermon was 'Lukewarm Christians Make Me Sick'.

Both men had a big impact on Tim. He comments,

Men need men to look them in the eye and give them a hard time. Both these men were strong and capable, and that was important for me. Most churches have more women than men, and I did wonder whether this was a feminine thing to be doing; women use a different language. I'm more of a muscular Christian; men need men. I came to see that the decision to follow Christ was not something to be embarrassed about, but to be on the front foot and challenge others about.

It was at this time that he began to live out what it means to follow Christ. He says,

Commanding a squadron of a hundred guys, you get to know them well. We were together seven days a week, and out on exercises constantly. I thought, 'You've made this decision to follow Christ, but what difference is it going to make? Are you going to live this out?' I was clear that my life should not be compartmentalised, and I never hid my faith. Everyone in the company knew I was a Christian, and there would be conversations with the men in quieter moments when they asked me about spiritual things – but I didn't preach at people.

Following Christ was life-transforming at the deepest level. It changed his understanding of his identity. He reflected,

Sun Tzu said, 'If you know the enemy and know yourself, you need not fear the outcome of a hundred battles.' And General Franks said, 'Commanders must understand who they are. An understanding of who you are is vital in leadership.' Having made the decision to follow Christ, I began to understand more about who I was. And to see that it wasn't just about me anymore.

It changed his view of what life was all about: 'My identity is in Christ and my purpose is to serve Christ. That is a very different perspective to just having a career in the military or in the City.' It changed his understanding of leadership: 'I wanted to be someone of deeper and better character. When taking people on operations, I wanted to love and serve them for who they are. I wanted to be a very good professional military officer – to serve the soldiers I was leading – and to earn the right to work alongside them and share the gospel with them.' It also changed his understanding of the role of the Army and the use of force:

> *Allowing evil to reign is not sweet innocence. While we live in freedom and democracy, the harsh reality is that large numbers of people exist under the thrall of non-democratic regimes and dictatorships, and the leaders of these regimes do not hesitate to use force as and when they feel the need. The bottom line is that pacifism isn't for me. I came to the conclusion that in the same way that we need a police force to enforce the law, using force if necessary to do so, there are times when the international community also needs to enforce the rule of law. It is not about whether God is on our side – God is not an Englishman or American. The real question is are we on his side? Are we aiming to use force in order to establish justice and righteousness, or to simply apply brutal power in conquest? I wanted to stand for justice and righteousness in the world.*

And so he did: during the Cold War, when posted in Germany, standing for freedom and democracy; on operational deployment in 1990/91 in the First Gulf War, when Saddam invaded Kuwait; and in the Balkans in the mid-to-late '90s, amid the horrors of ethnic cleansing. With regard to the latter, he comments, 'We were deployed on a peacekeeping mission, but there was no peace to keep. Serious damage was being done.' Therefore what was supposed to be peacekeeping quickly became a NATO enforcement operation.

It was as Brigadier in command of 101 Logistic Brigade in Macedonia, Albania, and Kosovo that he found himself faced with a humanitarian crisis. People had been told at night to be out of their houses by the following morning or be killed. And so they had fled – in their tens of thousands. They were mostly women, children and older people, the men having gone off to fight. Now they were in open country, in bad weather, with no food or shelter. At one level it had nothing to do with Tim and his brigade – they were there on a military mission to fight their way into Kosovo – but the brigade had the resources to help. And so Tim faced the decision put to him in that phone call: 'If I let these people in, can you guarantee you will look after them?'

He knew he couldn't guarantee this, but he also knew he couldn't just stand by and watch, doing nothing. Nor was there time to seek counsel from the MoD back in the UK. Tim remarks, 'My faith had a huge impact on making that decision and feeling comfortable with it.' And so the brigade spent the next few months building and running refugee camps. It was a decision for which he could easily have been sacked, but instead he ended up with a CBE for his response to the crisis. Now, two decades later, he still has people coming up to him in the street and thanking him for what he did: 'The best deployment ever,' as one such person said to him.

The faith that shaped his decisions is a faith that has also shaped his response to failure. The one that looms largest in his mind is the aftermath of the invasion of Iraq in 2002/03. Initially he was appointed the logistic component commander for the British forces going in to Iraq. That meant he was responsible for all the practicalities of moving the British forces and all their equipment. The initial plan was to move into Iraq from the north, which was a logistical nightmare. In the end the British forces decided to enter instead from the south through Kuwait, which was logistically more straightforward, so Tim handed his role down to someone more junior.

Newly freed up, Tim was asked to go to Washington as the British deputy in the US-led Office of Post-War Planning, and from there to Kuwait and Baghdad. Yet, as he describes, 'It was the first time I was to experience serious failure. I had been promoted very fast and been a general at just 49.' From the start of this role Tim was concerned about the lack of thought being given to what would happen in Iraq after the war. He said so – to very senior people. He was not afraid of speaking truth to power. He remembers lunch at the Pentagon with Donald

Rumsfeld, the then US Secretary of Defense, and a dozen senior US military personnel. Rumsfeld asked him directly what he thought. He replied, 'Militarily the plan is very good. We will win. But I'm concerned about post-war. We need to internationalise and involve the humanitarian world. And in the event of an insurgency we would need double the number of soldiers on the ground than is currently planned.' It was not what they wanted to hear. Their view was that they would get rid of Saddam, be applauded by the Iraqis, and the post-war would take care of itself. They could not have been more wrong. After the toppling of Saddam the country descended into chaos and years of being torn apart by some 40 different groups of violent militants.

He issued the same warning to the then Prime Minister, Tony Blair, at a briefing at Number 10, just before the invasion, as he later testified at the Chilcot Inquiry into the Iraq War. He says,

We talked for about 30 minutes. I was as honest as I could be about the position, essentially briefing that I did not believe post-war planning was anywhere near ready. I told him there was no clarity on what was going to be needed after the military phase of the operation, nor who would provide it. Although I was confident that we would secure a military victory, I offered my view that we should not begin that campaign until we had a much more coherent post-war plan.

It would be easy for Tim to point the finger, but he doesn't. He is all too aware of the difficulty of making decisions at the highest level. Not invading Iraq would have had consequences too. And he takes seriously his own responsibility for what went wrong: 'I asked myself, "What is my part in this? And what are the repercussions? Did I speak strongly enough, even if others say I did?"' He went on to examine biblical examples of failure and how people responded: Judas hanged himself for betraying Jesus; Pilate washed his hands of Jesus' fate; David admitted his wrongdoing in committing adultery and turned from it. Because of Tim's perspective on human nature from the Bible, he saw this as an opportunity to reflect on his own shortcomings:

> The British Army is deeply flawed because it is made up
> of people like me. I am deeply flawed. We all fail. None
> of us are perfect. We all make mistakes. And we need to
> be mature enough to recognise that. The answer is not to
> run and hide, but to ask, 'How can I grow through this
> and become a better man?' That way, having experienced
> failure, you come out the other end stronger.

As a Christian he can face up to failure, because his identity and confidence is in Christ. Tim says, 'When I meet the Lord, before his judgement seat, I have no defence other than Christ, because I am a sinful man. I don't say that lightly; it's just a reality. The essence of the message of Christ is very powerful for me.' But he hopes that final day may still be some way off, as he has plenty to do before then. Having retired from the Army in 2007 he now shares his time between lots of things he enjoys: academia as a visiting university professor, charitable work, business, and, until recently, politics, as the Army adviser to the UK House of Commons Defence Committee. But the common denominator running through this portfolio is what he calls 'morally courageous leadership'. He asks, 'What does such leadership look like today? How is it different to management? Where does character come from?' He is persuaded the answers lead back to one place, or rather one person – the man whose empty tomb had stopped him in his tracks all those years ago.

The challenge to be morally courageous is one that Tim puts not just to himself and other Christians but also to those who don't yet follow Christ: 'What is your purpose? What are you rooted in? Or are you just drifting through life trying to be a nice person? But actually that's not good enough. You can drift along aimlessly if you want, but this issue is pretty important. At least have the courage to face up to it and explore it.'

10

Cabinet Minister
Jonathan Aitken

Does going to church make you a Christian?

Jonathan Aitken had it all. As the great-nephew of Lord Beaverbrook, the son of an MP, and the grandson of a baron, he was from the right family. As the godson of Selwyn Lloyd – who served in Churchill's cabinet after the Second World War, and who took Jonathan under his wing and coached him after his father died – he had the right connections and mentors, and moved in the right circles. And with an address in the prestigious Lord North Street in Westminster, he lived in the right place, enjoying wealth and privilege. To all this he added the right job, with a career in politics that saw him rise to become Chief Secretary to the Treasury during John Major's term as Prime Minister, and to be mentioned as a potential successor at Number 10.

Jonathan had it all. And in an instant he lost it all – his career, his reputation, his money, his marriage. He suffered what he refers to as 'a royal flush of crises – defeat, disgrace, divorce, bankruptcy, and jail'. But what was a spectacular

131

fall *from* grace, as people refer to such things, actually became a fall *into* grace. It's been said, 'Grace, like water, always flows downward, to the lowest place.'[1] It was at that lowest place, in the darkest depths, that the amazing grace of God reached Jonathan, bringing new life and change: change in himself, change in his relationship with others, and most of all change in his relationship with God.

Before then, if asked, he would have called himself a Christian, but he now realises he was at best half a Christian, which he says is about as good as being half pregnant: 'I was one of those people who call themselves Christian without actually being one.' It wasn't as if he had had no interest in God at all. He had taken seriously his confirmation at school; later in life, when his twin daughters were born in difficult circumstances and he was told that all three ladies in his life were quite likely to die, he prayed hard; he went to church on Sundays, and on occasion did feel himself moved by a sermon he heard. He says of that time, 'Externally I could almost be described as a pillar of the Church of England.' But it was all very much on his terms. He sees it now for what it was – a wholly unsatisfactory, lukewarm, picking and choosing way of relating to God that had no impact on the person he was or the life he lived. He says,

The relationship I had with God was not unlike the one I had with the local bank manager in the country town where I grew up. I knew he existed, that he was a person of some importance who was to be respected. I spoke to him

politely, visited his premises intermittently, occasionally asked him for a small favour or overdraft to get myself out of difficulty, thanked him condescendingly for his assistance, kept up the appearance of being one of his reasonably reliable customers, and maintained superficial contact with him on the grounds that one of these days he might come in useful. The fundamental fault line was that I thought I was in charge of the account. There was no obeying, no surrender, and a complete disregard for the walk of the Christian faith. I felt I could do it my way.

He considered himself not a bad person, although he sometimes did bad things. As for the prospect of death and judgement, he reckoned it would be 'alright on the night with bank manager God' – not that he ever reflected much on such matters, thinking himself at the time to be immortal. The superficiality of this nominal faith was reflected in his thoroughly worldly aspirations: 'When I was a young, ambitious politician, I followed the somewhat cynical advice in these lines by Alexander Pope: "Get place and wealth, if possible with grace. If not, by any means get wealth and place."' And get them he did.

After graduating in law from Christ Church, Oxford in 1964, he became a Fleet Street journalist. He was a senior reporter and feature writer for the *London Evening Standard*, serving as a war correspondent in Vietnam, Biafra, and the Middle East. After journalism he went into business and became Chairman of a merchant bank in the City. Then in 1974 he became a Member of Parliament. In

1992 he was appointed Minister of State for Defence, and then joined the cabinet two years later as Chief Secretary to the Treasury.

The defence job involved huge responsibility, which he relished. The entire armed forces were built on the premise that the Soviets were coming, but after the collapse of the Soviet Union it was clear that the Russians weren't going anywhere. Thinking about how to reshape things strategically and militarily was a vast and intellectually demanding exercise called 'Frontline First'. Jonathan was the architect. He comments, 'Bringing together the military and civil service and intelligence agencies was a thrilling episode. It was a big task. They don't come along like that in life very often.'

It was his promotion to the cabinet however that confirmed he had now arrived as a serious player at the top table of British politics, and he was understandably elated. He explains,

I was being given one of the most fascinating and powerful jobs in government, for the Chief Secretary to the Treasury is the controller of Britain's £300 billion public expenditure budget with a remit of responsibility that extends across all Whitehall departments, agencies and committees ...

I was riding on the crest of an exciting career wave, which in a sea of tired cabinet colleagues seemed likely to take me onwards and upwards to still more powerful positions.

But little did the surfer know how abruptly and finally the ride was about to come to an end. The rocks on which he would be dashed came in the shape of a libel case.

In addition to speculations in the media that he was a future Prime Minister, there were also allegations in *The Guardian* that he was a pimp, an illegal arms dealer, and a corrupt minister who had amassed a huge fortune from his secret connections with prominent Saudi Arabians. Confident he could disprove the charges, he launched a libel action in the High Court, in the course of which it was proved he had told a lie on oath about who had paid a bill for his stay in the Ritz Hotel in Paris in 1992. He says, 'All hell broke loose. I was on the front page of every newspaper. My life was in ruins.' The subsequent campaign to have him prosecuted for the crime of perjury lasted for the next 18 months. Although it was a period of total disaster in which he lost everything, it was at the same time marked by a spiritual journey which led to a new life of commitment to Christ.

The first step on the journey was that of self-examination. As he describes, 'I asked myself fundamental moral and spiritual questions about how on earth I managed to make such a mess of things and lose my spiritual moorings and anchors.' It didn't take him long to find the answer. The title of the first volume of his autobiography says it all: *Pride and Perjury.*[2] As he puts it,

> *Pride was the root of all my evils. Without pride there would have been no libel action; no attempt to defend the Ritz bill*

payment with a lie; no will to win the battle in court on an
ends-justifies-the-means basis … If I had been blessed with
a small helping of humility instead of possessed by a surfeit
of pride, the entire tragedy would have been avoided.

He recognised it as a particularly strong temptation of high office: 'Politicians are especially vulnerable to this. As Defence Minister you've got guards of honour saluting you. You think you can walk on water. Pride blinded me. And of being in the cabinet, or moving higher, one motivation was various forms of pride.' He realised that pride had not only led to this downfall, but had also alienated him from God: 'Pride puts such a roadblock between yourself and God. It is, as C.S. Lewis described it, "the complete anti-God state of mind".'

Facing up to this truth about himself determined his response to the perjury charge. He says,

I reached the point fairly quickly of seeing the magnitude
of my own sin. I didn't waste time arguing about that,
even with myself. If I had pleaded not guilty, there was
a 60% chance or more of getting off because of huge
technicalities in the law. Perjury is extremely difficult to
prove. And a good few people were urging me not to give
myself up and instead to roll the dice. But I knew I had
done wrong and I pleaded guilty.

This acknowledgement of wrongdoing before others and before God marked the beginning of his journey to faith in

Christ over the course of the next 12 months. He describes it as a bumpy ride with many twists and turns:

> *There was no big, dramatic, single moment of conversion. It happens to some. For me it was a more difficult and painful journey: stumbling, falling, sinning, backsliding, wondering if it was true or not and whether I was going crazy. But there was momentum. It was like travelling across Europe by train at night. You don't know when you crossed the frontier, but you do know when you have arrived.*

Some of the most significant stations on this journey were interactions with Christians who came alongside him out of the blue, albeit sometimes in the most awkward and embarrassing way. It began with a Christian ringing his doorbell one day and asking if he could come in and pray with him, given he was going through such a terrible time. Jonathan comments, 'Belonging, as I did, to the "church reticent" wing of Anglicanism, I would rather the earth have swallowed me up than pray out loud.' But it was to be the first of many such visits by this man and his friends to give prayer support. Before long they urged him to attend a Christian enquirers' course at their church. Jonathan recalls, 'I could not have been more reluctant. I had known all about Christianity for years, and sitting around in groups is not for me. But I came to see that there is a distinction between knowing about God and knowing God.'

On the first evening he was surprised by the high quality of the talks, and that his group had some interesting people in it, including some clever tax lawyers, but he had no intention of returning. However, not having a better invitation, he found himself back there the following week. It was in the fourth week that he was particularly struck by a talk on how to pray in which the speaker gave lots of practical tips on prayer. Jonathan says, 'When I got home I thought I'd maybe give it a try. Almost immediately it changed my non-existent prayer life, and in time my whole life.' This beginning of prayer was to lead him in due course to praying to receive Jesus Christ into his life as his rescuer, who died for his wrongdoing, and as his ruler, who was raised from death as Lord.

The cynic might see his story as a classic example of a foxhole conversion, with faith in God being nothing but a psychological crutch in a crisis. Jonathan observes, 'The cynical side of myself worried about that at the time too. Was I using Jesus as a crutch and religion as a way out of the mess? I was in frightful trouble and found God. How very convenient.' But he rejects this charge, not only because of his core belief and conviction that the message about Jesus is true, but also because the path of following Christ was in many respects harder rather than easier for him. He adds, 'I do not believe that this fundamental change came about because I was seduced at a time of weakness by "the consolations of religion" ... because what followed my commitment to deeper faith was not consolation but an almost unbearably testing vocation.'

The fruits of his faith in Christ became evident in three main areas. Firstly, there was upward change, in his relationship with God. He says, 'Somewhere along the painful road of the journey I recognised that I had accepted Jesus into my heart as my Lord and my God.' His receiving of Christ gave him in turn an assurance of his own acceptance by God. He continues, 'I feel I am at peace with God, and that is a great feeling to have.' And this new relationship with God brought about a fundamental change of direction in life. He wrote, 'Having made the commitment to God, I now look forward to following him wherever he leads with trust, hope and joyful acceptance.'[3] That is a commitment which continues to this day and which he sums up in a recent letter: 'I hope I have moved from the self-centred life towards the God-centred life. Continuing along this road is today my life's purpose and philosophy.'

Secondly, and flowing from this, there was outward change, most notably in his relationships with others, beginning with his nearest and dearest. He describes, 'Within the family all sorts of new and enriching horizons opened up as I had more time and willingness to share my fears, frailties, and insecurities.' At the root of this outward change was a new dynamic of living for Christ. Therefore, despite his inadequacies, he can declare: 'The result is lots of unseen small things, for example in how I treat other people, as well as other charitable works.'

Thirdly, there was inward change, starting with the simple question of who he was. He explains, 'For me it was an essential self-interrogation after falling from a mountain top of political power into a mine shaft of media opprobrium ... In the end there was only one response to the question "Who am I?" with which I could live. It was: "I am a sinner who wants to repent."' One of the biggest inward changes was a sense of peace which he hadn't known when his star had been rising as a politician. He wrote,

> *The more my career prospered on the surface, the more my deeper feelings were signalling an emptiness and lack of fulfilment within ... Gnawing away at me inside was a problem I could not describe, except by giving it psychobabble labels such as 'lack of inner peace', 'emptiness of feeling', 'hollowness of spirit', or more simply 'something missing'. It was as though, after spending a lifetime wanting to climb a particular mountain, I had unexpectedly reached the final approach to its summit only to discover that there was nothing there worth the effort of the ascent.*[4]

The contrast with his state of mind shortly before going to prison could not have been greater. He wrote at the time,

> *By all normal expectations I should be apprehensive, depressed, on the edge of a breakdown, tormented by pressures and turmoils, hating my enemies and despairing of my future. Yet I am in none of these moods. Instead I am calm, contented, tranquil, often joyful, full of love for*

my family and friends, and brimming with positive hope
for the future.[5]

But that sense of peace was about to be severely
tested. *Porridge and Passion*,[6] the second volume of his
autobiography, begins with his account of 8 June 1999.
The day dawned with his butler pulling back the curtains
in Jonathan's bedroom, pouring out a cup of his favourite
Jamaica Blue Mountain coffee, and hanging up the suit
he had just pressed. Camped outside the front door in
Lord North Street were at least a hundred photographers.
Jonathan wrote, 'Eighteen hours later my evening ended
less comfortably. I was perched on an iron bedstead inside
a cell at HMP Belmarsh, drinking tap water, nibbling at
a stale bread roll and listening fearfully to my fellow
prisoners chanting obscene threats about what they were
going to do to various parts of my anatomy.'[7]

That afternoon he had stood in the dock of Court One
in the Old Bailey and listened to the words, 'I sentence you
to 18 months' imprisonment. Take him down.' He had
blown a kiss to his teenage children and elderly mother
before being taken down to the cells, driven off in a white
police van, and then left in the caged reception enclosure
of the prison. As he describes, 'It was a wild scene. A
panorama of anger and despair. One young man who was
hysterical was charging into the bars of the cage, with
blood pouring from his head. Another was overpowered
by six wardens as he tried to escape. Muscled men were
crying with their heads in their hands.'

The induction process was not however without its lighter moments. In his interview with the prison psychiatrist he was asked the standard question, 'Does anyone other than your next of kin know you are in prison?' Thinking a touch of humour might be appropriate, and knowing that his sentence had not gone unnoticed by the great British public, he replied, 'I think perhaps 15 to 20 million people know I'm in prison.' The psychiatrist must have been one of the few people not aware of the identity of prisoner CB9298 sitting before him. After a pause the man said, 'May I ask you, have you ever suffered from delusions?' Later that evening any sense of amusement quickly evaporated however as he sat in his cell listening to the chanting about him echo across the jail. He recalls, 'Nothing had prepared me for the venom, the viciousness, and the intended violence of this chant. I was terrified … I do not think I have ever felt more lonely, more frightened, or more vulnerable.'[8]

He tried to pray, but was so scared that he couldn't even say the Lord's Prayer. It was then that he remembered a well-wisher at court earlier in the day had given him a calendar-style booklet titled 'Praying the Psalms'. For that day the reading was Psalm 130, which begins, 'Out of the depths I cry to you, LORD'. The words made an immediate impact:

A warm and comforting wave of reassurance flooded over me. Suddenly I realised that I was not as lonely, scared, helpless, or vulnerable as I had thought. The author of the psalm had been there before me. Some 3,000 years earlier he had experienced very similar emotions of despair to mine. He had found a route to climb out of his depths with God's help and he had signposted that route in beautiful poetry.[9]

Inspired by this, Jonathan made it a regular part of his routine from then on to ponder and pray over two or three psalms each day, as he would later share in his book *Psalms for People under Pressure*. He writes, 'The results of this discipline were amazing. While in jail I found myself continuously grappling with an onslaught of problems. They came in three categories – immediate, external, and spiritual … A love of the psalms helped me to liberate and quieten my soul.'[10] But no-one was more surprised than he was to find himself soon praying and reading the Bible with other prisoners. It all began with him writing a letter.

On Jonathan's third day in jail a young prisoner came to him for help, being unable to read a letter he had received. When Jonathan not only read it to him but also wrote a reply, the young man left his cell holding the letter in the air and calling out, 'That MP geezer, he does fantastic joined-up writing.' With a third of prisoners being unable to read or write, Jonathan says the commercial fell on the ears of a receptive audience, and from then on he had queues forming every evening outside his cell door. Through his letter writing he got to know prisoners and made friends. One of them was an Irish burglar called Paddy.

He recalls that it fell to Paddy one day to say thank you to him on behalf of the lads for all his help, which he duly did by offering him for free anything he wanted from his extensive collection of hardcore porn magazines. After a fleeting moment of temptation, Jonathan declined the offer with this explanation: 'These days I'm trying a different path in life – following Jesus Christ. I've been on it for some time now, and it's making a big difference to me.' Paddy responded, 'I'd really like to try that path for myself. How can I get on it?'

The floodgates opened and out poured a torrent of questions and worries, the gist of which was that he didn't know what life was all about and none of it seemed to make any sense, but that his grandmother used to believe that Jesus 'stuff' and her life did have meaning. Jonathan asked if he would like to say a prayer with him. At the end of their session Paddy decided that this was too good to keep to the two of them. Jonathan writes, 'Paddy, who had in him the qualities of a good recruiting sergeant, decided that our two-man prayer partnership needed reinforcements to help in this crisis. So in double quick time he persuaded a blagger (armed robber), a dipper (pickpocket), a kiter (fraudster), and a lifer (murderer) to join us.'[11]

The group, which soon grew in size, came to be characterised by a number of 'P's – pain, prayer, perseverance, penitence, power, and peace. Jonathan explains:

The misery of imprisonment meant no-one was playing games pretending pain was not real. In prayer they started to communicate with God, and to persevere in that. Penitence is the idea of repentance. In Greek the word means a complete change of mind and heart leading to a change of life. The test of whether it is genuine is the fruit. There was all sorts of fruit in that prayer group of anything from 6 to 20 people meeting every night in jail to talk, share, read the Bible, and pray. The changes were significant: stopping swearing, throwing away porn, being civil to pariah prisoners and to prison officers, making restoration to victims, getting in touch with families, breaking the drug habit, and fighting to stay clean. This was big stuff in prison life.

Jonathan was in no doubt that these changes could not be attributed to sheer willpower. He says, 'Secular teaching about how to get off drugs talks about needing a higher power. But whose power? That is left dangling. The answer is the power of the Holy Spirit. They wanted the power of the Spirit to come in and change them.' And he did. One result was peace:

It's hard to describe but you can see it and feel it. Young aggressive guys started to settle down and be different people. And it lasted. I know what happened to the 20. When I got remarried, the media pointed out that the same number of ex-prisoners as ex-Cabinet ministers turned up to the wedding. Of the 20 some 16 were going straight. Something must have happened in that prayer group.

The most devoted and passionate member of the group was Paddy himself: 'He threw away his porn, stopped swearing, became a good prisoner, got in touch with his wife, wrote to his victims, and fought and won his battle against heroin addiction. He has given his life to Christ and is still on that path today.'

The change that faith in Christ brings has proved lasting in Jonathan's own life as well. Now 18 years on he is still following Christ in what he calls the 'unending adventure of walking with God'. He says, 'The best way to get to know God is to immerse ourselves in his Scriptures,' and so he spends time each day reading the Bible and praying. His current favourite Bible passage is the end of Isaiah chapter 40, which says, 'those who hope in the LORD will renew their strength'. He can testify to the reality of that. And he is as committed as ever to living out this relationship with God on the ground, be that in charitable work in prison reform and rehabilitation, or in writing and speaking, or in any of the other activities of his new life.

When Jonathan's life began to fall apart back in 1997, he received a letter from Charles Colson. Colson had been Special Counsel to President Richard Nixon and was imprisoned in the 1970s for his part in the Watergate scandal. He wrote,

> *You can let circumstances shatter you, or you can decide that adversity will be your greatest blessing … As you know I have looked back on Watergate and thank God for it. Through that crucible I came to know Christ personally*

and discovered that in the darkest moments of my life He was working to produce what I would later see as the greatest blessings of my life.

Jonathan made the same discovery. Although initially he was full of bitter regrets at his crass errors of judgement and character, and was cross with God, he now looks back with a different perspective. He comments, 'I thank God for his rough chastening, because without it I would not have found relationship with God and all the blessings that flow from that.'

When he tells his story, he often begins with a health warning: 'Don't confuse the narrator with the hero.' The hero of the story is not Jonathan but God, whose grace brought new life and change. Of the many books he was written, one is a biography of the former slave trader John Newton who wrote the hymn 'Amazing Grace'. Although Jonathan says he himself is not worthy even to touch the garment of that great man, he can relate to his experience of the transforming power of God's grace. He explains, 'I was blind and deaf to the real message of repentance and judgement and love and transformation. I used to think it was just ritual rather than a life-changer. I was blind but now I see.'

The opening of his eyes was a painful process in which he lost everything in worldly terms. At the lowest point of his humiliation he was declared bankrupt and stripped of all his worldly goods. He wrote, '*The Guardian* appointed a Trustee in Bankruptcy whose first actions were to remove my wristwatch, my cuff links and my son's computer.' But he continued, 'I may have lost the whole world of my previous life, but I have found my soul in a new life.'[13] He adds, 'Having lost all place and wealth, I was guided to the path of God's grace.'

Of his new life, seeking to serve God rather than himself, he says, 'Despite all my obvious faults and failings, it is my relationship with a loving and forgiving God that has made this possible. This is why the glory of his name and of the transforming power of his love has become the greatest of my new passions.' He feels now as Paddy did all those years ago, that this news is too good to keep to himself. And so he hopes and prays his story might lead some to respond as Paddy did and to say, 'I'd really like to try that path for myself' – or at the very least to find out more. It is a path Jonathan describes as 'the best journey in the world'.

11

Insurance Executive
Richard Borgonon

Why should I bother with the Bible?

There's insurance and there's insurance. The first type is the bog-standard, common or garden, billy basic, everyday stuff you take out for your car, house, home contents, and health. It's jolly useful when things go pear-shaped, but, that aside, let's be honest: it's pretty dull. It's never going to set the world on fire. The second type of insurance is Lloyd's of London. This is what you need when someone has set the world on fire. Lloyd's is one of Britain's oldest institutions and is the world's leading specialist insurance and reinsurance market.

Lloyd's insures big things – ships, for example. That's where it all began back in 1688 when Edward Lloyd's coffee house became recognised as the place to get marine insurance – for very large container ships and their cargo, and cruise ships. Unfortunately the Titanic was one of theirs. The payout for that one came to the then princely sum of $10 million. But Lloyd's also insure other big things that (like the Titanic) don't float, and that (unlike the Titanic) aren't supposed to – planes, satellites, and other objects that hang about in space (such as Richard Branson's Virgin Galactic private spaceship for tourists). They insure art too (including Leonardo da Vinci's cartoon 'The Virgin and Child' in the National Gallery) and expensive jewellery (such as Elizabeth Taylor's 69-carat diamond ring, which the policy specified she could only wear in public for 30 days a year, and that while protected by security guards).

They have also been known to insure rather more unusual things: David Beckham's legs, Ken Dodd's teeth, and Bruce Springsteen's voice. If 'the Boss' were to damage his vocal chords such that he could no longer perform, Lloyd's would be facing a $5 million payout. Their customers include not just celebrities but the multinational corporations and governments driving the global economy.

It is with this Lloyd's type of insurance that Richard Borgonon deals. In fact this has been his world for the past 40 years and more. But as a senior insurance executive he has an unusual sideline: he reads the Bible with people. To be more precise, he reads John's Gospel with other senior insurance executives – lots of them. At the last count he was meeting one-to-one with some 20 of them. What's even more intriguing is that these movers and shakers in insurance who read the Bible with him are not Christian. No-one is more surprised by all this than Richard himself. If you had told him a decade ago that he would be doing this now, he would have laughed – very loudly. But a single dinner changed everything. It all began with a meal he had one evening with two people – one was a Professor of Mathematics from Oxford University, and the other was the most powerful insurance broker in London at the time. What happened that night was to reset the course of Richard's life.

The first day he pitched up at Lloyd's he received nine job offers. He was just 19 and it was an industry starved of young people, so he turned down the chance to go to university and began work there instead. By 29 he was the youngest main board director of the most successful privately held broking business in Lloyd's. By 51 he was Chairman of one of Lloyd's broking firms, and one of four broking industry reps on the Market Reform Group that determines how the insurance industry in London is to operate in the future. He had dealt with some of the largest insurance contracts ever, such as 65% of all the medical malpractice insurance for hospitals in the Western States of the US. He had also chaired 14 specialist insurers, including the biggest writer of sports and leisure insurance in Europe and Australia.

But the road to the summit had not been without its bumps. In his early 30s he was on a business trip to the States when he was infected by a very nasty brain virus. He was off work for almost a year and wouldn't be fully fighting fit again for another eight years. He was on medication throughout this time and had to fly to the States a week ahead of any business meeting so he could acclimatise. He remembers in the early days sitting at home with two baby daughters in his arms and being unable to string a sentence together. Yet he was also aware of other arms holding him. He says, 'I was conscious of being in the arms of a loving heavenly Father. God used this time, and through it my faith in him was deepened.'

This concept of a personal relationship with God had been totally alien to him when he was growing up. He comments, 'I was brought up on churchianity not Christianity. It was classic man-centred religiosity. It was all about religious services.' His father had been the chief cantor for the Gregorian Society. Richard's light-bulb moment came in his mid-teens. He describes, 'At the age of 15 I was on a New Year conference with another church, and I learned for the first time that it wasn't about churchianity but about Jesus Christ. And it wasn't about what I was doing but about what Christ had done in dying for me.' It was only after his mother died, years later, that he found she had made the same discovery. In a diary she kept, the last entry read, 'How wonderful it is to understand grace. How I had thought it was all about what I had to do, rather than what has been done.'

Religion, which demands you try to pay your way to earn God's favour, weighs you down with a heavy burden. It is very bad news. By contrast the message of what God has done for us in Christ is called in the Bible 'the gospel', which literally means 'good news'. William Tyndale, the 16th-century pioneer translator of the Bible into English, described it as 'good, merry, glad and joyful news that makes a man's heart glad and makes him sing, dance and leap for joy'. And, we could add, that also makes you want to share it with others – which is how Richard found himself at dinner with the professor and the broker.

He and the broker were good friends who inhabited the same world of insurance and classic car racing, but when it came to matters of God and faith they were on different planets. His friend was highly sceptical of anything Christian, but happy to discuss and fire out his questions. The time came when Richard thought it best to wheel in the heavy artillery. It doesn't come much heavier than John Lennox – Professor of Mathematics at Oxford, and internationally renowned as a speaker on the interface between science, philosophy, and religion, who has gone head to head in televised debates with the likes of Christopher Hitchens, Richard Dawkins, and Peter Singer.

Two dinners and seven hours of discussion later, the friend was loving it all, enjoying the intellectual stimulation of debate with someone with a brain the size of a small planet, but Richard felt they were getting nowhere. The professor would give brilliant answers, but the broker would just come back with yet another question. The problem, as Richard saw it, was that his friend didn't know the first thing about what the Bible says, because he'd never actually looked at it. Richard decided enough was enough, and told his friend straight, 'There's no point in carrying on with these debates. For the first time in your life you've found something you know nothing about it. You're biblically ignorant. We're not doing this again unless we get the good professor back next time to show you what the Bible actually says.'

And so they did. For round three the professor brought with him to dinner a copy of John's Gospel. They spent the evening looking together at the first 18 verses, which Richard describes as an executive summary. It begins, 'In the beginning was the Word, and the Word was with God, and the Word was God. He was with God in the beginning.' Although sceptical about the idea of God creating, the broker was intrigued by this figure called 'the Word' who 'was with God', and surprised that God was presented as a personal being rather than a force. By the time they reached verse four, the man – who was known in the industry as 'Golden Tonsils' because of his gift of the gab – found his jaw on the floor when he read, 'In him was life, and that life was the light of all mankind'. The astonishing claim is that Jesus was the eternal Word who came into the world as a man; he was the creator of life and everything, and the way to God for all humanity. Then there was the equally astonishing offer in verse 12: 'Yet to all who did receive him, to those who believed in his name, he gave the right to become children of God'. What for the broker had just been intellectual curiosity and something of a game was being replaced by wonder at what the Bible actually says and a desire to find out more.

Sadly he left the country that very week and moved to Bermuda, but it had been an eye-opener not just for the friend but for Richard as well. He had seen the power of God's living Word silence London's most powerful insurance broker, and he didn't need to see that twice to be convinced that he must take this same Word to his other friends. And so off he rushed to see his local church minister, William Taylor, asking if he would please teach him how to share John's Gospel with others, and the two of them began meeting up to go through it.

Richard himself was no expert in such things so he took copious notes. Also, as in his line of work he might have 15 business meetings in a day, there was no way he was going to remember anything of what he was being taught in these preparation meetings unless he wrote it down. But there was another point to the note-taking as well. He explains, 'In every business meeting I was in there would always be a contract or an agenda or a presentation which both parties would study. So if I was going to take this to my friends, I needed exactly the same – two sets of identical notes, with the Bible passages included, that we could then study together.' When Richard began to offer his friends the opportunity to look at John's Gospel together the take-up was immediate, and he soon found himself doing lots of these one-to-one studies. It snowballed from there, and before long demand was such that the notes were published for wider use as *The Word One to One*.[1]

The comedian Lee Mack once said on the radio show *Desert Island Discs*: 'If an alien came to earth and asked if there was one book he should read to understand humanity, I would tell him it was the Bible. But as to what it says, I've no idea. I've never actually read it. So I'm looking forward to reading it on my desert island.' What Richard discovered among his peer group of senior insurance executives was a similar attitude – ignorance of the Bible and a desire to change that – but also a willingness to take action now rather than waiting until they were castaways.

Richard's invitation typically goes something like this:

The Bible is the most published book in the history of our world. Haven't you ever thought you might one day take a look at it? Wouldn't you expect that it might have some good stuff in it, even answers to life's big questions? Well I've got some really helpful notes that take just one book of the Bible, which starts with an executive summary. Can I buy you a coffee so we can look at this overview together? It's just 18 verses. All I'll say to you at the end is, 'Did you enjoy that? And would you like to meet again to see what happens next?'

He's not asking people to sign up to anything. It's not a course. It's just taking a look at a Gospel with the help of some notes. Not everyone takes up the offer, but a lot do. There's no pressure exerted, but it's become well known now in the City that this is a useful thing to do. He's found that senior executives who wouldn't be seen dead in a public group setting admitting their ignorance are comfortable reading the Bible with a friend one-on-one.

Some common themes have emerged. Many of these men used to say all roads lead to the same God, but Richard found that 9/11 opened up a huge crack in their world view: they realised they certainly didn't believe in the God of the radical Islamists, and they were suddenly more open to reading the Bible. He then kept coming across the admission: 'I am not at peace.' For some it was that they had it all – the money, the status, the sports car, the luxury SUV, the holiday villa – but found it didn't give them what they were after. For others the lack of peace was because they didn't end up with the toys and health and relationship they had hoped for.

But in more recent years the mantra he has heard most is: 'I don't feel secure.' For some it's the breakdown of faithfulness in relationships, not least in marriage, or it's the fear of terrorism, or Brexit, or jobs not being for life, or even just retirement. As one of them put it, 'For our parents' generation it was different facing retirement. They looked forward to going to the Seychelles. We've already been there. And facing retirement you feel lonely and fear losing your identity.'

The specific reasons that these senior men (and as a married man it is just men that Richard meets with) are happy to give it a go reading the Bible vary widely. One 50-year-old managing director said to Richard after a year of meeting up,

> I never told you why I agreed to start meeting. My father died of cancer when I was just 15. He was a committed Christian who had been very senior in a Christian charity. I was angry with God for the next 35 years for taking my father, but I couldn't forget the peace and radiance my father had so clearly experienced as he faced death. He

*was going home. He had something I don't have, and from
reading John's Gospel I now know what that was.*

Another man, who runs his own company, for two years
declined the offer to meet. Then one day Richard received
an email from him with a single line: 'The time has come
to look at the notes.' He later explained, 'I was in the gym
on the treadmill, and I suddenly realised that I'm 49, on the
treadmill of life, and haven't a clue where I'm going. I need
answers. There's probably some good stuff in the Bible, so
it's time I looked at it.'

A company chairman also refused initially, saying, 'I've
heard you're doing this, and I think it's a good thing, but
it's just not for me.' Sometime later they found themselves
at the same business meeting. The man walked into a
room full of people, pointed at Richard, and said, 'You
were right and I was wrong. I need to see you.' He turned
to the others in the room and continued, 'Richard offered
me something I didn't think I needed, but I was wrong.'
He explained afterwards, 'I was on my knees gardening
at the weekend. It suddenly struck me that I've lost two
friends to cancer, one friend to a heart attack, and another
to a brain aneurism in the last year. I'm 62 and haven't a
clue what I believe. I should probably start having a look at
your notes.' He loved what he found there and has come
to trust in Jesus for himself.

Another individual, who was one of the most powerful
men in the industry, with a crazy-busy diary, set aside an
hour at 8 a.m. every Monday to meet. He came to faith

in Christ, and is now meeting up with the 'on my knees gardening' chap to study together.

It's impossible to predict the response to the offer to meet. Richard made his pitch with some trepidation to one particular highly successful but tough and difficult character: 'You may have had religiosity in your upbringing, but I bet you don't know true Christianity.' He asked Richard to repeat what he'd just said, which he did. The man then started to cry. He explained, 'As a child I was abused by a Roman Catholic priest at school. I became an alcoholic and had no end of trouble in relationships. In AA I was told to entrust myself to a higher power. But I've never been comfortable with something so vague. If this book might have some answers, let's start.'

Not all of these people come to faith in Christ through their reading, but to a man they say at some point, 'Why has no-one ever shown me this before?' It's a good question. What they discover is invariably quite different to what they had assumed. A common misconception Richard encounters time and again is that through your life you are essentially building up a file for the interview at the Pearly Gates. It is precisely what Richard himself used to think. The idea is that at this interview you will hand over the file which makes the case for why you should be let into heaven. It might start with a letter of introduction from your mother, saying you've always been a good son; an Excel spreadsheet listing every last penny of your charitable giving; a reference from your company about the kind of boss you've tried to be; a note from your wife and children about your efforts to be a good husband and father; a cover letter from yourself about how you've done your best and are a good deal better than Stalin or Hitler. Richard explains what a shock it is to then read Jesus saying in John chapter 5 verse 23, 'Whoever does not honour the Son does not honour the Father who sent him.' Yet what a relief to read in John chapter 3 verse 36, 'Whoever believes in the Son has eternal life', and to realise that it's not about what we do, but about what Jesus has done for us – and personally trusting in him and his death for us.

Many have done just that. One of them was the international chairman of one of the biggest insurance groups in the world, whom Richard describes as one of the brightest men he's ever met. The man said,

> *The first six words of John's Gospel – 'In the beginning was the Word' – were like a branding iron on to meat. I couldn't get them out of my head. There has to have been a beginning to everything and here was the claim that the Word had done it all. I came to see who the Word was, what he had come to do by becoming a man and dying on the cross for me, and that through him I could come to know God personally.*

He added, 'It was nothing you said, Richard – it was what the Gospel said!'

The discovery that many of these senior insurance executives have made is one that many others of all ages and stages are now making around the world as the published notes have gone global. A Hindu woman attends a lunch in a bank in Hong Kong, and through reading John discovers how she can be made right with God. She in turn reads it with her 74-year-old father. With tears rolling down his cheeks he realises that he isn't tied in to an endless cycle of reincarnation, and he accepts Jesus as his rescuer and ruler. An Iranian businessman walks into a church in Sydney, proclaiming, 'I've read the Koran – it's all rules. I now want to read the Bible.' The man on the door offers to read John's Gospel with him. Now three months later the businessman has just been baptised. His brother, whom he brought along to interpret, is getting baptised this summer, along with his wife. And his mother has started coming to church to find out what on earth is going on.

A 78-year-old widow starts reading through John's Gospel with her friend's 91-year-old housebound mother. The friend's mother knew she was not at peace. Now she is, having come to faith in Christ. A young, bubbly blonde takes the notes away to go through with her brother. Her church minister comments to Richard, 'I buried her father, her mother is an alcoholic, her brother a drug addict. A friend went through John's Gospel with her. She now believes in Christ and is reading John with her friends at school.' A 13-year-old boy discovers Jesus through John's Gospel, and the change in him is so marked that he is now sharing the booklets with his parents. From the iconic Lloyd's building in the City of London to the corrugated huts of the townships in South Africa, the same words are having the same impact, as people are reading the Bible for themselves and discovering what it really says.

Richard once met a Chinese woman who told him that when the missionaries were expelled from China, they left behind their Bibles. She said,

My family ended up with a section of one of these missionary Bibles. They thought the paper of such fine quality that they took it apart and used it to wallpaper a room. But when they finished they started reading what they had put up and came to faith in Jesus. I am now the third generation to come to faith through the Bible room in the house.

For those who are not so keen on the redecorating option, the Bible and *The Word One to One* John notes are available on the Internet for free!

Now 61 Richard hopes to have many more years of sharing the good news of Jesus and encouraging others to read the Bible for themselves, but he's aware that time is short and the stakes are high. He comments,

This life is like a click of the fingers. In a nanosecond we're gone. And what then lies ahead is eternity. Nothing matters more than sorting out where you truly stand with God, and seeing that it's not about what you do, but about what Christ has done for you. John's Gospel is written so 'that you may believe that Jesus is the Messiah, the Son of God, and that by believing you may have life in his name.'[2] Surely, at the very least, that has got to be worth the investment of taking a closer look!

12

Fashion Leader
Simon Ward

What difference does Christian faith make at work?

It's not every day you come across a 60-year-old dressed in cherry-red Dr Martens, matching leather jacket, and a black and white palm print shirt. But then what would you expect from a leading figure in the fashion industry? Simon Ward was until recently Chief Operating Officer of the British Fashion Council. Fashion gets its fair share of bad press, associated in the minds of many with child labour, sweat shops, sexual exploitation, and vanity. As such it may seem an odd place for a Christian to have spent his working life and an odd thing for a Christian to be passionate about. But Simon is convinced that God shares his passion for fashion. Rather than God and fashion being at odds, his Christian faith helps him understand why fashion matters and how the fashion industry can be run in a way that addresses its destructive side and harnesses its power for good.

Although brought up in a Christian home, it wasn't until his early 20s that Simon came to a personal faith in Christ. He says, 'I was dragged along to church until my 13th birthday, at which point I was given the choice and did a runner. Faith in God just hadn't engaged with me.' Through his teen years he developed swearing into a fine art, even writing his own manual of swear words. But his older brother was a keen Christian, who kept praying for him and would meet up with him when they both moved to London. He gave Simon a Bible and other books to read, and discussed with him. It was when Simon moved back to live with his parents for a while that he started going back to church with them.

His motives were far from spiritual. He didn't have a girlfriend at the time and the prospect of a couple of hundred young people at the new church his parents had joined sounded too good to ignore. But although he went along for the girls rather than for God, it was on a weekend away with the church that things fell into place for him spiritually. He recalls, 'The message about Jesus seemed totally logical and such a compelling solution to what life is all about – where we've come from and where we're going. It seemed to me to answer all the questions. And Jesus struck me as hugely attractive. I opened the door of my life to him. In he came and off we went.' But off where exactly would not become clear for a good while, at least not on the work front.

'How many failures can you fit into one life?' asks Simon with a wry smile, looking back on numerous false starts.

Yet positively his perspective is that 'failures are not failures because they are part and parcel of who you are and how you are developing. Own it and move on, and see it as part of the journey.' He failed his A-Levels first time round, and didn't do much better the second time. His father was in the Navy, so Simon decided he would go into the Army, but they didn't want him. He did a geography degree because he thought it best to do something fairly general, given he didn't know what he wanted to do. He loved opera and had a good voice, so tried his hand at that, with initial encouragement from his Italian girlfriend's opera-mad father. Over the course of 12 years he sang 26 of the great tenor roles in operas on the edge of the professional world, but although he had the voice to make a career of it, he never managed to get it sufficiently under control. His final performance was that of Don Jose in *Carmen* in the Embankment Gardens under London's Charing Cross station. He says,

> As I prepared to enter through the audience I looked up at a statue. It was Robert Raikes, founder of the Sunday School Movement. It was a classic example of God's sense of humour, as I then ended up running the children's work at my church for two years. During that time I managed to persuade them to appoint a director of children's ministry, thinking they would employ me. They chose somebody else!

Alongside all of this, to pay the bills while he was pursuing singing, he got a job in fashion. He started out in the menswear department of Selfridges, the highlight of which was measuring the inside leg of Bruce Springsteen one afternoon. He went from there to the British Clothing Industry Association before moving to the British Fashion Council in 1986. He never really intended to get into the fashion industry, but that is where he ended up spending his working life. And he's done rather well in it. Without ever applying for a job he found himself being promoted to Head of Operations, then Joint CEO, and finally to Chief Operating Officer.

To appreciate the significance of the British Fashion Council (BFC), a bit of context helps. Fashion is the 15th biggest industry in the UK, contributing £26 billion to the UK economy and employing almost a million people. It is big business, and on the world stage Britain is a big player. London is one of the big four fashion capitals alongside New York, Milan, and Paris. Simon explains, 'Fashion is something at which Britain leads the world. We've got the most envied high streets; our colleges are indisputably the best, attracting students from every continent; and our designers attract an international following that brings a spotlight on Britain. What goes on in the UK fashion industry has global significance.'

At the epicentre of all this is the BFC, which was set up in 1983 to further the interests of the British fashion industry. It is the BFC that puts on London Fashion Week, which twice a year for men and women brings together the top designers, providing them with one of the world's main fashion showcases. Although Simon is modest about his achievements, to have worked at the BFC over the past three decades and enjoyed a leading role there means that he has been right at the heart of the action in terms of global fashion.

The world of fashion sounds very glamorous, and he admits that there is that side to the work. He comments, 'With the position I've had, I've got to meet an awful lot of VIPs in all sorts of grand places.' But that isn't what excites him. He adds, 'I don't care about the hype and celebrities, but rather the designers and the story behind their work.' Part of his work over the years has been encouraging young designers and supporting new talent. One of the early initiatives he was involved in was to give six young designers – one of whom was a young man called Alexander McQueen – a room at the Ritz for free to set up their clothes and meet people. Simon says, 'Most young designers who would later become well known – people like Julien Macdonald, Matthew Williamson, Jasper Conran, Betty Jackson – would come to see me because I was the person who looked after the support schemes, and I got to know all of them fairly well.' He would meet with them, give them honest feedback, encourage them, and talk through options. His view was: 'There is only space for a very few designers, so it's important to respect people and be real with them.'

What he loved most about working with the designers is the creativity: 'The creative process is something which, every time I come across it, face to face with the designer, I find really stimulating. I guess it takes you back to how

God looks down on the world. He created the world and all its creativity, and you're encountering that creative process.' As humans we are creative because we are made in the image of a Creator God. And just as God's creativity is expressed in beauty and infinite variety, so our own creativity should give expression to the same beauty and variety, not least in fashion. Simon explains, 'God created seasons with variation, and he made 60,000 species of trees. He made an extraordinarily creative and varied world, and so it would seem to me to be rather turning our backs on his creativity if we were just dressed up in the same white T-shirt every day.'

The Bibles emphasises the importance of growing in godly character, and that God is more concerned for what is going on in our hearts than about our appearance, but it would wrong to conclude that externals don't matter. The way Simon puts it is: 'Inner character is where you start and invest most,' but then, he continues, 'Fashion can help us then express our identity and character. We need to move away from image, which is about dressing to impress, and think instead of dressing to express.' These are issues Simon is going to be encouraging young people to think through as he takes workshops in schools around the country next year. He also points out,

Clothing is both a requirement and an opportunity to recognise different circumstances and to convey trust and respect. It is part of negotiating life's journey. Would you turn up to a wedding in a T-shirt? Would you expect a

workman at your door in a sharp suit or in jeans? Would
you relax at home in the evening in your suit?

But Christian faith, as well as giving a foundation for understanding the value and significance of fashion, also has plenty to say about the darker side of the fashion world. Initially the teaching Simon took on board from church about what it means to be a Christian in the workplace was quite generic – not fiddling your expenses, working hard as for the Lord, and not gossiping. It was only when he started meeting up with other Christians who worked in fashion that he began to think through with them how Christian faith relates to issues specific to the fashion world. Out of this the organisation Fashion for Christ was born, founded by a friend of his in the fashion world, Chrissie Abbott, and joining its bigger sister Models for Christ. The question that crystallised in Simon's mind was this: 'If God were the boss, how would he run the fashion industry?'

He's certainly not claiming Christians are the only ones trying to tackle the abuses in the industry, but Christian faith gives a clear mandate for addressing them and has energised and informed his own efforts. One example is the problem of the industry predominately employing skinny models, which hit the headlines again in 2008 when two South American models died of anorexia. He explains, 'The fashion world can be brutal. Models might be flying in from New York overnight. They then face the possibility of rejection at castings. Fittings can be unkind.

And because models are tall for the catwalk, if they are young then they tend to be stick-thin. If God were the boss, how would he run things?' An enquiry chaired by a member of the House of Lords was set up and changes introduced to provide better care and support for models – no under 16s were to be allowed on the catwalk, and proper food was to be provided backstage, together with counsellors for models.

Another issue is justice in the supply chain. He gives an example:

In 2013 more than a thousand people lost their lives when a multi-use factory collapsed in Bangladesh. The previous day cracks had started to appear and structural engineers were called in. Whereas others workers stayed away the following day, the garment factory workers went in because of tight deadlines for Western retailers. Add to that the pitiful amounts the workers get paid, all so that Western consumers can enjoy infinite choice at low cost, and the injustice of the system is glaring.

The Bible has lots to say about justice and how we treat the poor. Simon has therefore been doing what he can and using his influence, together with others, to ensure a more just supply chain and that people are paid a living wage for their work.

In addition there are environmental issues. Simon says, 'One tonne of cotton takes 400 tonnes of water to grow it, untreated dyes may be released into rivers, arsenic is used in tanning leather, and so on. In the UK there were issues such as unpaid internships, which was common practice in the fashion industry.' Simon was at the forefront of looking at alternative solutions, ensuring that interns were paid for the work they do. With all these issues he has kept coming back to the question of what God would do if he was running the industry. Drawing on his 35 years of experience working within the fashion sector, he has also now written a book exploring this, called *The Character of Fashion*.[1] It includes his list of 'God's Ten Commandments for Fashion' which sum up what he thinks God's priorities might be if he were in charge of fashion.

Although he has now stepped down from his day job at the BFC, his enthusiasm for exploring the difference Christian faith makes on the ground in daily life shows no signs of slowing down. 'Now I've finished my apprenticeship!' he says with a wink and a smile. A visit to Holy Island in North-East England a few years ago sparked his interest in the psalms, as in centuries past the monks who were based there used to memorise all 150 of them. Inspired by this Simon had a go at memorising 15 of them on his cycling commute to work. He wrote down his reflections, now published in a book called *Riding the Tide*,[2] exploring how these ancient prayers relate to 21st-century life. The musical side of him, which almost led to a career in opera, is also finding new expression. He has recently released a CD, *Declare His Glory*, setting every word of ten psalms as contemporary songs. Various other projects are on the boil.

On his website he introduces himself by saying, 'I'm on a journey and I'd like to share it with you. The journey's called life …' As he looks to this next stage of his journey, he takes inspiration from older Christians he knows who are really going for it in living out their faith. He adds, 'There's nothing more attractive than older people who are looking outward. Anna the prophetess in Luke chapter 2 was 84. I heard the retired bishop Michael Baughen speak movingly about suffering after the death of his wife. He's also 84. I've got a quarter of a century more to go. C'mon Simon!'

13

Opera Singer
Jacques Imbrailo

Aren't Christians hypocrites?

He has performed in many of the big venues – the Royal Opera House in Covent Garden, Carnegie Hall, Wigmore Hall, the Zurich Opera House, and the Concertgebouw in Amsterdam. He's worked with the big conductors – Sir Mark Elder, Vladimir Jurowski, and Sir Antonio Pappano. He's sung with the big singers – Jonas Kaufmann, and Ferruccio Furlanetto. He's ticked off the baritone dream roles – Billy Budd, Pelléas, Don Giovanni, and the Count in *The Marriage of Figaro*. At 38 Jacques Imbrailo seems to have done it all.

The reviewers are impressed too. 'Imbrailo aced it. With consummate stage awareness, musicianship and skill, he turned every singer's worst nightmare into the stuff of dreams,' proclaimed *What's on Stage*[1] following his performance of the title role in *Don Giovanni* at the Glyndebourne Festival Opera. 'Jacques Imbrailo is the finest Billy I have heard – lusty, virile, sensitive and moving,' wrote the *Financial Times*[2] about an earlier Glyndebourne appearance. *The Guardian* agreed: 'a total joy – slight, lithe and wonderfully guileless, singing his farewell to life with immense dignity and pathos.'[3] Wherever he sings, he makes a big impact: 'the star of this performance'; 'one of the great interpreters of the title role'; 'sensational from beginning to end'; 'dominates the stage'; 'to witness it was a privilege'; 'on Elder's recording of *The Apostles* it is the young South African baritone Jacques Imbrailo, in the role of Christ, who has won the most praise'.[4]

That last quotation, from a review in the *BBC Music Magazine*, goes on to say this: 'Elder believes that, quite apart from his glorious singing, Imbrailo drew strength from his own deep Christian faith.'[5] It is a faith that is central to who Jacques is. As another reviewer observed, 'Jacques Imbrailo's faith comes first – if necessary, at the expense of his career.'[6] Phenomenally successful he may be, but he is clear about where his priorities lie. He says, 'I'm a Christian before I'm a singer.'

He got into singing really by accident. As a boy he had enjoyed music, and would sing his homework to memorise it, but he never had the discipline to learn an instrument. Growing up on a farm in South Africa, he was more into wrestling. He was disqualified from his first bout – aged six – for biting his opponent's finger, but went on to win three South African championship medals. Singing came a few years later when a choir visited town and Jacques and his friends dared each other to audition. His mates ran off, finding the tall English conductor too scary, but Jacques stayed on and got in. And so aged 11 he went off to the Drakensberg Boys' Choir School. He explains, 'I didn't grow up in a musical house so my time at that school was my first exposure to classical music. During my four years there I learned to love Mozart, Bach, and Handel, and was introduced to a number of great composers. I think that was where my love for classical music began.'

The other significant musical influence on him was Professor Werner Nel, the Head of Music at Potch, his South African university. Jacques comments, 'I went to university to study law and took singing lessons with him as a hobby. His passion for lieder and opera was hugely inspiring. Through his wonderful teaching and encouragement I went on to do a music degree and subsequently came to the UK to pursue a singing career.' He won a scholarship at the Royal College of Music, and then a place on the Jette Parker Young Artists Programme at the Royal Opera House. His first major public recognition was winning the Audience Prize at the 2007 Cardiff Singer of the World Competition. Three years later he was singing the title role in *Billy Budd* at Glyndebourne. It was to prove a career-defining part.

The Christian faith that now so defines him predates his singing:

The message about Jesus is something I have believed ever since I heard it as a young boy – that we have gone our own way and are in the wrong with God because of it; that this relationship needs to be fixed and we can't do it ourselves; that God in his love sent Christ to take our wrongdoing on himself in his death on the cross; that if we trust in Christ, this restores our relationship with God. I had plenty of questions as I grew up, but I knew it to be true. The gaps were filled in as I got older.

Growing up in South Africa Jacques knew plenty of people who professed to be Christian but whose lives told a very different story – the Bible labels such hypocrisy as a dead faith that cannot save you – and by contrast he knew others for whom it was real and was lived out in everyday life, not just on Sundays. He was determined back then, and still today, to be the real deal:

Following Christ impacts on every aspect of my life – how I relate to my wife and kids, how I interact with people at work, and how I act on stage and deal with mistakes. It has to be part of all of your life. It has to influence how you think and make decisions. In my interactions with my wife I want to be more Christ-like, and that's how I want her to be too. It's the same with my kids. I fail miserably all the time, but that is my goal.

Following Jesus shapes Jacques' approach to his work in all sorts of ways. For starters it means there are red lines he won't cross. As one reviewer put it, 'Jacques Imbrailo may be the hottest young baritone on the block but, as a committed Christian, he's not about to go down the "barihunk" route: shirt off, rippling muscles celebrated as much as the bruising vocal gymnastics. Putting his faith first, the young South African singer knows exactly what he will and won't do for his art.'[7] Jacques explains, 'I certainly wouldn't take all my kit off on stage. I don't feel comfortable with that. If it's harmful to my wife, Cara, or other Christians, I've got to ask, "Is this the right thing to do?"'

But the impact of his faith is more than just not doing certain things. Positively it means seeking to put God first in everything. He says, 'Before I go on stage I ring my wife and ask her to pray for me. And I pray in my dressing room that I'll do a good job, that I'll deal with it in the right way if things go wrong, and that I'll perform for God's glory and honour, not my own.' The Bible is clear that we were made to live for God and to have him in the centre circle of our lives. Putting anything or anyone else in that centre spot, even something good, turns it into a false god. Jacques is all too aware of how easily this can happen in his line of work: 'Singing is a very difficult industry to make a success unless you are very committed. The competition is so big, with more singers than opportunities. You have to sacrifice a lot and are away from home a lot.' If you're not careful, it can take over your whole life. He recalls meeting a young singer who was just starting out and saw singing as everything in life. Jacques' reply was, 'Singing is wonderful, but it's just a job. It's not something I couldn't live without. I love being at home with my wife and kids.' His family have a rule that he will never be apart from them for more than three weeks at a time.

The other way singing can become a false god is by allowing it to become your identity. Jacques comments,

The voice is a very personal instrument, so it's easy to have a mindset of 'I am a singer – it's my identity'. And you're constantly being praised or criticised, so it's easy to let that determine who you are. People are nitpicking all the way through rehearsals, and then there's the applause and reviews after the show. You can get swept up by it all. But my identity is in Christ. I'm a Christian before anything. And I remind myself of that through reading the Bible and talking to other Christians.

Should he ever let it all go to his head and become diva-like, his wife and kids quickly bring him back down to earth with a bump and keep him grounded.

His determination that music should not become his idol does not mean however that he is lacking in passion for what he does. He loves music. He remembers the first time he sung Bach's *St John's Passion*, as a boy chorister, he was overcome by the beauty and complexity of the music. He sees music and singing as wonderful gifts from God for us to enjoy and celebrate, and he feels their power: 'Music has the ability to move us very deeply. It resonates with us. Films without music would be very bland.' He adds, 'Singing is unusual in that your instrument is inside you, which is both frustrating but also hugely satisfying when your voice does what you want it to.'

Singing has a long and important tradition in Christian thinking. The book of Psalms is a collection of 150 songs which were sung by God's people in the Old Testament temple and accompanied by musical instruments. The Bible calls us to praise God in song, and that is something which is part of any church service today. But even if singing has a central place among Christians, some people might question the value of opera and doing that as your job. Jacques admits there have been times when he's wondered if it is worthwhile and worth the sacrifice of being away so much from home, but the bottom line is he believes it is.

He was just nine when he saw his first opera and it made a huge impression on him. The woman in the lead role as Madame Butterfly was a lady of considerable size but playing a character who was supposed to be tiny. Somehow she made it believable. It was his first exposure to the power of opera. As a child he loved watching TV and imagining how he would think if he were the character on the screen. Now he gets to do that as his job on stage. It's largely a solo lifestyle with a lot of time on his own, but that suits his personality – he's reserved yet likes expressing himself in performance.

In some circles opera has a bad press, being seen as only for the elite few. Jacques' response is that many new operas are in English or French or German; there are subtitles in most opera houses giving a translation; and even if you don't understand directly what is being said in the librettos (the text of the opera), the music does a lot of the emotional talking and expresses the text so you can keep up with the story. As for the ticket prices he comments, 'It's an expensive art form to put on, with 100 or so people on or around the stage who need paying every night. But even so the prices don't cover the cost of the performance. It couldn't survive without sponsorship from the government or private sector.' With regard to the value of opera Jacques argues,

> Opera brings beauty and release from everyday life. It also reflects life and tragic situations, with stories about love and betrayal and crises and death. The characters, even if at times taken to extremes, ring true with everyday situations in our lives. We recognise that we sometimes feel as they do. Opera can illustrate life and emotions to a heightened level with the power of music.

As a reflection of life, art depicts both the good and the bad. This means that often Jacques is playing characters whose values and lifestyle are at odds with his own beliefs as a Christian. It's something he's had to work through. Don Giovanni, for example, is a thoroughly un-Christian character living for wine and women, who has seduced hundreds, refuses to repent, and ends up in hell. But when Jacques was considering this role, someone helped him see that by playing the character really well and making him as believable as possible, people would see how unattractive and destructive such a lifestyle is. The other perspective that helped him was recognising how hypocritical it would be only to play the good guys. He remarks, 'I am rubbish myself. It's not that I'm good and they're bad.' The seeds of all these wrong things are in every human heart.

Some roles however are more problematic. With Don Giovanni it's clear-cut that the character is in the wrong, whereas that isn't the case with, say, Pelléas. Jacques explains that Pelléas is something of a niche role because not many baritones can sing it. Given Jacques can, he's already performed the lead role three times and has five more in the pipeline. But as a Christian he finds it a challenging one to do. Pelléas is a young man who falls in love with his brother's wife. In the opera he is portrayed as innocent and encourages sympathy, whereas Christian values uphold the importance of faithfulness in marriage.

But as well as reflecting the darker side of life and relationships, opera can reflect the good, as in Britten's *Billy Budd*. Performing the title role at Glyndebourne in 2010 at the age of 31 gave Jacques his first big break and kick-started his career. It was very well received and got a Grammy Award Nomination. Since then he has played the lead role a further four times. The story is about a sailor called Billy who is sentenced to death. He sacrifices himself by forgiving the captain, who could possibly have saved him by pardoning him due to the circumstances of his crime. He also saves the ship by accepting his punishment, even though it seems unfair to his shipmates, and by urging them to follow his example of forgiveness. In this he is portrayed as a sacrificial lamb, laying down his life like Christ to save others. The big difference though is that Christ, unlike the flawed and legally guilty Billy, was totally innocent and perfect. In other pieces the biblical links are more explicit, as in Elgar's *The Apostles*. Singing the part of Jesus in that was a moving experience for Jacques. He comments, 'It brought home to me the love and care of Jesus, and also the level of suffering he had to go through – not just being crucified but bearing the punishment we deserve.'

As for the future Jacques says, 'Roles change as you get older. You're not going to get a 50-year-old singing Billy Budd, whereas Germont in *La Traviata* is better sung by an older voice. A baritone voice matures late and reaches its peak aged 45–55, and can last even to 65 or 70.' Jacques therefore has plenty of singing to look forward to. But his horizon stretches beyond that to the return of Christ and eternity. In the light of that perspective, life now is not unlike being in the dressing room, a place Jacques knows well. At the Royal Opera House in Covent Garden he typically arrives in his dressing room two-to-three hours before the show starts, does some stretching, warms up his voice, puts on his costume and then his make-up, looks through the music, chats to colleagues, and reads through the director's notes from the previous performance. He gets a half-hour call, a five-minute call, and then a final call when it's time to go on. As a Christian, although life now is a wonderful gift to be lived to the full for Christ, there's also a sense in which you're in the dressing room, waiting for the curtain to go up and the main show to begin, when Christ returns.

Jacques sums up it up like this:

Christ is going to come again. Our purpose is to glorify him in how we live our lives, and to tell other people about him so they can be saved. This present, flawed creation is aiming somewhere. I want to be prepared for the end when Christ comes – to make sure I'm ready and keeping going in a personal relationship with Christ, and becoming more like him. I want to take care of my family and encourage them so they too are saved when he comes again. That day will either be one of great fear or great joy for people. I want it to be one of great joy for myself and my family, and those around me.

The need to be ready reminds him of an incident early on in his career that still makes him shudder. He was on the Young Artists Programme at Covent Garden and was covering one of the lead roles. On one particular day he was told it was certain he wouldn't be needed for the evening performance as the lead singer was strong as an ox and in good health. That evening Jacques checked his phone at 7.30pm, the time the performance started, saw there was no message, and turned his phone to silent as he went into a prayer meeting at his church. When he switched it on again at the end of the evening he found thirteen frantic voice messages from the Royal Opera House. The baritone had not told anyone that he was unwell until he walked on stage. He only sang the first half, refusing to sing the second. Mercifully a legendary singer just happened to be on hand and stood in to sing the role from the side of the stage, but it was a lesson the young Jacques learned the hard way. As the head of casting made clear to him the following day, not only do you need to stay within six miles of the Opera House when you're covering, you also always need to be ready for the call. It's a mistake he has never repeated in his work, and it's one he doesn't want to make with God. And so given we don't know when Christ will return, Jacques is determined to live each day ready to meet him.

14

Directors' PA
Yvonne Edwards

Where can I find freedom from addictions?

Yvonne has spent the past decade working as a high-level PA for boardroom directors in financial services, latterly at the Financial Conduct Authority. She says, 'Every day is an onward journey of allowing Jesus to be the master of my heart. I try to be humble and gentle and demonstrate my Christian faith, living it out and being consistent in the workplace. And I feel very comfortable with expressing openly that this is such a big part of my life.' Those are remarkable words from someone who for many years wanted nothing to do with God.

Her father was one of 10 children and her mother one of 11, both from Roman Catholic families, but by the time Yvonne arrived her dad was an atheist. Despite this she was sent off to convent schools and as a young girl accepted that what she was being taught from the Bible was true. This childhood faith didn't last long. She began to detect differences between what was practised and preached, and by the age of 10 this hypocrisy had left her determined to have nothing more to do with church as soon as she could decide for herself. She explains, 'I became the teenager from hell. I couldn't wait to leave home and remove myself from parental authority. By my mid-teens I had come to the conclusion that everything I'd been taught was nonsense. I threw out God, along with the Tooth Fairy and Father Christmas, and became an ardent atheist.' Rejection of God can be expressed with the drift of apathy or the fist of hostility. With Yvonne it was the fist. She continues, 'I was an angry atheist. I had a violent internal reaction to any mention of God or even any thought of him. Whenever anyone referred to God or *Songs of Praise* came on TV, I felt an uncontrollable antagonism and anger.'

Her atheism was accompanied by hedonism, as she abandoned herself to the pursuit of pleasure without boundaries: 'I discovered men, relationships, drugs, alcohol, and partying. I loved everything that had had a "don't" in front of it. It was great fun. It was the law of forbidden fruit.' Her search for excitement took her to South America, where she became involved with a semi-famous racing driver and enjoyed a lifestyle of eating at the best tables in the best restaurants, taking cocaine, and drinking like a fish. It was a 'live hard, die young' approach to life which led to the death of a good friend of hers at the age of 32 from substance abuse. But this shot across the bows did nothing to dampen Yvonne's enthusiasm for excess. She became involved in less and less healthy relationships, four of which ended in broken engagements.

It was during this time that drink really started to get a hold on her, and the gap grew between the person she was on Fridays at 7 p.m. and on Saturdays at 2 a.m.: 'Once I started I couldn't control it. It began with fine wines and champagne, but I became less discerning as the years went on. I loved vodka because I thought people couldn't smell it on you. But I was resilient, strong, stubborn, and managed to hold a job down and earn a decent living.'

Having returned to the UK Yvonne realised that her friends were all getting married and settling down, and that the 'wild child' image wasn't appropriate for her now as a 30-year-old. So she took what she sees now, looking back, as a 'selfish decision' to get married. She comments, 'Mercifully the man I married happened to be a lovely, honest, decent man, quite unlike any of the boyfriends I had been involved with over the years. He was also hard-working and successful, so I was financially secure. Life was good – lovely house, striped lawn, and trips on Concorde and the Orient Express.' But the arrival of their first child triggered a rapid downward spiral in her drinking.

She already had one child from a previous relationship at the age of 23, but back then he had been little more than an accessory, like a handbag, and her life had just carried on unchanged. When her second child came along she stopped working and stayed at home. Until then she had been driven by work, which had at least provided some structure to life and put boundaries around her drinking. Once this constraint was removed, chaos quickly followed. The tiger she had been riding turned on her. She explains,

My drinking took on mammoth proportions and moved to a whole other level. I wasn't just getting drunk in social settings; I started drinking on my own at home. My husband would find me drunk when he came home from work.

He arranged for Yvonne to see a doctor, but she just spent hours getting herself ready before the appointment and lied through her teeth when she got there about how much she drank. She remarks, 'The doctor was totally taken in by my cover-up. His recommendation was to try and stick to wine and beer, and not to drink before 6 p.m. In fact I was so good at pulling the wool over people's eyes that he even wrote to my husband that "Mrs Edwards is a charming woman" and thought it must be him who had a problem rather than me.' But behind the charming, glamorous façade, things were going from bad to worse.

To cut off her access to drink Yvonne's husband cut up her credit cards, but she got around this by turning to what is called 'non-beverage alcohol'. This means drinking anything with an alcohol percentage sign on it – whether it was her husband's after shave, something else in the medicine cabinet, or even things stored in the garage. By this stage cracks started to appear in the well-kept veneer, with her skin turning a shade of yellow and the silhouette of her tall, slim figure becoming painfully thin, except for the bump of her protruding abdomen – her distended liver made her look pregnant.

Her family decided enough was enough and booked Yvonne in with Alcoholics Anonymous. She says, 'The people were nice, but they mentioned God. Inside I was bristling with antagonism and anger. I couldn't believe anyone could be so foolish as to believe in God.' She made a big effort to keep up appearances, but as one lady at AA observed, 'The shop window looks nice, but what is going on in the stock room?' Her comment made Yvonne furious, but she knew the woman was right and that she had seen through her. Nevertheless Yvonne stuck with it and went along to the sessions for the full three months, and by the end of the course had stopped drinking. Life seemed to get better – yet it wasn't to last. She soon felt bored, wanted the fun back, and started drinking again. Before she knew it she was not only back to square one but worse than ever. She reflects,

> I'm optimistic by nature and had always been a 'glass half-full' person – in more ways than one – but a terrible feeling of darkness and loneliness came over me. Although I had a lovely home and wonderful husband and children, I fell into a deep depression. It was an awful and lonely place to be. People would tell me, 'If you loved your children, you would stop drinking for them.' But I couldn't, even though I did love them so much. I would collapse into bed at night and didn't want to wake up in the morning. I wished I wasn't here anymore.

Eventually these suicidal feelings led to her taking a massive overdose – everything in the medicine cabinet. Mercifully Yvonne's life was saved by a neighbour who happened to call by and found her before it was too late. She was rushed to A&E and had her stomach pumped.

Thanks to her husband's financial means, she subsequently found herself booked in to The Priory, the private psychiatric hospital in South-West London famous for its treating of celebrities. Yet as Yvonne explains,

> *I wasn't facing reality. I felt like Kate Moss! The grounds were lovely and the chef cooked for you whatever you wanted. I was sober, didn't have an overwhelming urge to get alcohol, and by the Friday I was bored. I was the only patient in there for the alcohol and drug programme, and everyone else had gone home for the weekend.*

It was the August 1995 Bank Holiday. Yvonne remembers it well because that weekend was a turning point in her life, as she goes on to describe:

> *I had been out for a walk in the grounds, thinking about life and about things I had heard about God in the past. I went back to my en-suite room and opened the bedside drawer, hoping to find a copy of* Vogue *or* Cosmopolitan *or* Hello! *to flick through. Instead all that was there was a Gideon's Bible. I picked it up, opened it at random, and started reading. It was Luke's Gospel chapter 7. I read from verse 36 to the end of the chapter.*

The passage describes an encounter between Jesus and a prostitute who comes to him while he is at dinner in a Pharisee's house. (The Pharisees were a strict religious group in the first century who prided themselves on their observance of God's laws.) Weeping, the prostitute anoints Jesus' feet. The woman is painfully aware that she is a 'sinner'. Yet the self-righteous Pharisee is appalled that Jesus would allow such a woman to touch him. In response Jesus tells a story about two debtors. One of the debtors owes 10 times as much as the other, but neither has the money to repay. The moneylender graciously cancels the debts of both of them. Jesus then asks, 'Now which of them will love him more?' The Pharisee answers, correctly, 'The one who had the bigger debt forgiven.'[1] Jesus then explains that this is the reason for the woman's behaviour. She loves Jesus so much because she knows that her debt of sin – that Jesus has cancelled by forgiving her – was so huge. By contrast the Pharisee has little love for Jesus because he is blind to how sinful he himself really is.

The impact on Yvonne was immediate. She continues,

Suddenly I was overwhelmed with a sense of my own sinfulness before a holy God. It just came on me. As I read this account I realised that my whole life had been lived in rebellion, running away from God. He had given me the gift of life and health and family and home, and I had done all but destroy it while ignoring him. This was my debt before God. But I also saw Jesus' love and forgiveness. I got down on my knees and at the age of 35, for the first time, bowed my head to something bigger than me and my ego with its pride and arrogance. I surrendered my will and my life to God. I said, 'I'm sorry. Sorry for the terrible, sinful, rebellious, hedonistic life I've led. Please forgive me and help me.' I was crying – real tears.

She knew there and then that God had answered her prayer:

I had a strong sense of God's presence with me. It was as real as if I could see him. And I felt truly at peace. At peace with God and peace in myself. Until then I had never known peace apart from circumstances when all my ducks were in a row. Now I had true inner peace. I wasn't on any medication. I knew the experience was real, not drug-induced.

She didn't know what to do next though. She was afraid that, in a psychiatric hospital, if she told anyone they would think she was mad. And she was afraid that if she went to sleep, she might wake up to find the experience had disappeared. So as Yvonne went to bed she kept talking to God, praying, 'God, please don't leave me.'

When she woke up the next morning the sense of God's presence was as strong as ever. She was also healed of her alcoholism:

Although I was incredibly thin, I looked five months pregnant because of my enlarged liver. But when I woke up that morning, the swelling had gone and everything

had returned to its normal size. I remember touching my
tummy in amazement. And from that day my alcohol
problem was history. I haven't wanted or needed a drink
since, and don't even think about it. It was a miracle. Like
the gospel accounts of Jesus healing people of leprosy, it
was just taken away.

And so that weekend a new life began of following Christ
and of freedom from alcoholism. It has been a life of
purpose and growth, but not without its challenges. The
reaction Yvonne met at home was mixed. Her husband
was pleased she was now sober, but he also wanted back
the girl he had married, even though in her view that
girl had been nuts. Yvonne says, 'He could see that I had
changed, but he put it down to all the money he had spent
on my treatment at The Priory rather than to God. I had
assumed he would want to become a Christian, but he was
apathetic. He wasn't antagonistic, but rather just had no
interest in God.' Sadly 10 years later, in September 2005,
he had a massive heart attack and dropped dead on the
squash court.

When Yvonne started out as a Christian she knew very
little and was hungry to learn. She explains, 'I just wanted
to learn more about God and get to know him better. I had
great enthusiasm for God because of what he had done
for me.' One day at the school gate she met a woman who
was a minister's wife, and she started going to their church
on Sundays as well as to midweek prayer meetings and
Bible studies. It was there that she took the step of getting

baptised and making a public profession of faith in Christ. She has been an active member at the church ever since.

Twenty years on she is as overwhelmed by the love of God towards her as she was that night back in The Priory when, reading about a woman whose debt of sin had been wiped out by Jesus, she came to experience for herself the transforming power of Christ's forgiveness.

Epilogue

Isn't Christian faith just a psychological crutch?

The psychological crutch

Some dismiss God as a delusion. They claim that people have come up with the idea of God to help them cope with life and to meet their psychological needs for hope and meaning. They claim that he doesn't exist except in the minds of believers, and that faith in him is just a psychological crutch for the weak and needy, of whom Christians are a prime example.

Some who dismiss the Christian faith in this way see it as a dangerous delusion. For the atheist Richard Dawkins it is a virus in society that needs wiping out. The late Christopher Hitchens claimed it poisons everything. Others see it as harmless delusion and are happy for Christians to believe in their imaginary friend if it helps them, as long as they keep their views to themselves.

Aldous Huxley, in his novel *Brave New World*, pictured a society of the future in which people were kept happy with their lot in life by a state-produced drug called Soma.

It was said to have: 'All the advantages of Christianity and alcohol; none of their defects … take a holiday from reality whenever you like, and come back without so much as a headache or a mythology.' And so the idea goes that life is hard and people have different ways of escaping reality. Some escape into an imaginary world on the screen – the virtual world of computer games, or endless TV box sets, soap dramas, or entertainment shows. Some escape from reality through alcohol or drugs. Some use the state-sponsored escapism provided by the National Lottery. Some escape through immersing themselves in the arts. And Christians allegedly escape through their belief in God and heaven. It's pathetic but harmless, like a child believing in Father Christmas or fairies at the bottom of the garden. Anyway, some say, because of their faith Christians actually do a lot of good in society, not least through voluntary work, so let them have their delusion.

But the question of whether or not the God in whom Christians believe actually exists really matters. Firstly, it matters for Christians because following Jesus can be a costly business. Many Christians around the world pay a very high price for their faith in Christ. They are driven from their homes, rejected by their communities and families, imprisoned, tortured, and killed. No-one wants to pay that kind of price for a lie, for a delusion, for faith in a God who isn't actually there. Even for those of us who are not living in such situations of persecution, the call of Christ is to turn from living for yourself, take up your cross, and follow him. It's not the easy option. And anyway, regardless of the cost, life is too short and precious to waste it believing a fantasy.

But secondly, this question also matters because of the implications if Christianity is true. If it is, the consequences are massive – for everyone. It means there is a God who is actually there, and we were made for relationship with him. It means people are not living with him as God in their lives as they ought, and will one day face him as judge and be justly alienated from him for ever. It means that God in his love sent his Son Jesus Christ to die for us and our wrongdoing, and that through him we can enjoy eternal life and forgiveness instead of condemnation. There's an awful lot at stake if it is true. So the question really matters.

Real psychological needs

The next thing to recognise is that as human beings we have real psychological needs, and Christian faith does meet those needs. Firstly, as humans we have a psychological need for love. If there is no God, then the universe feels a very lonely, hostile, cruel, and cold place. Yet what a difference to life if you believe there is a God who is a loving heavenly Father, who cares for us so much that he sent Jesus to die for us, and through this to rescue us for relationship with him. But is this Father figure actually there or not?

Sigmund Freud was the most famous advocate of the view that belief in God is just a psychological crutch. He wrote about religious beliefs, 'They are illusions, fulfilments of the oldest, strongest, and most urgent wishes of mankind ... The terrifying impression of helplessness in childhood aroused the need for protection – for protection through love – which was provided by the father ... Thus the benevolent rule of divine providence allays our fear of the dangers of life.'[1] He was claiming that God is a projection of this desire we have for a father figure to care for us and provide the love and protection we experience from our parents as children. But in his view this heavenly Father figure exists only in people's minds. Was he right?

Secondly, there's the psychological need for hope. The atheistic perspective on life is that the universe and life exist just by accident, and there is nothing beyond death, so when we die we rot. It's bleak. What a difference it makes if you believe, as Christians do, that death is not the end, and that what lies ahead is life for ever with God and his people in a world made new, without any suffering or pain or wrongdoing or death. Karl Marx famously claimed, 'Religion is the opium of the people' – a drug that gives you relief from the pain of life in this world, especially for the poor. Well there's no doubt that Christian faith does relieve the pain and bring comfort. But is what it promises real or not?

Then, thirdly, there's our psychological need for meaning in life. If the atheist is right and there is no God, then there is no ultimate meaning to life. It is meaningless. Pointless. We're just a few chemicals in bags of skin, lost in space, frantically running around on some speck of dust for 70 short years, filling our time with things of no ultimate importance, until we become food for worms. One of Samuel Beckett's plays is called *Breath*. There's a pile of rubbish on stage. The light that illuminates it starts off dim, gets a bit brighter, and then becomes dim again. All you hear is the cry of a baby, then some breathing, and then a final cry. And that's it. The end. The whole thing takes about 35 seconds. It's a bleak view of life – that we're just rubbish, here for a few brief moments and then gone.

By contrast, what a difference Christian faith makes. Life then does have meaning. We were created for a purpose – to know and love and serve God. We know who we are, and where we've come from, and where we're going, and what the point of life is. With God the big questions of life are answered. But is that faith in something real or in what we just wish was there?

The list of psychological needs goes on – the need for morality and absolutes; the need for there to be justice in the end; the need for peace for our troubled conscience. All of us can relate to these psychological needs and desires. They are needs which belief in God does satisfy, as the stories in this book testify. That makes faith in God very attractive. But does that belief correspond with reality or is it just a psychological crutch?

False psychological claims

A couple of points are worth noting. First, the psychological crutch argument seems to assume that because faith in God satisfies psychological needs, it must be a delusion. But why so? That faith in God works is exactly what you would expect if God exists. If he is there and we were made for him, it makes perfect sense that knowing him brings peace, purpose, hope, meaning, and wholeness.

Secondly, the atheist should beware assuming they themselves are free from psychological influence. There are psychological reasons for wanting God to be there, but there are also psychological reasons for not wanting him to be there. Not believing in God has certain advantages. It means there's no ultimate authority or accountability, so you can live as you want. That is very attractive to us as people who want to do our own thing.

The atheist philosopher Thomas Nagel acknowledged,

I want atheism to be true, and am made uneasy by the fact that some of the most intelligent and well-informed people I know are religious believers. It isn't just that I don't believe in God and, naturally, hope that I'm right in my belief. It's that I hope that there is no God! I don't want there to be a God; I don't want the universe to be like that.[2]

Aldous Huxley wrote, 'For myself, as no doubt for most of my friends, the philosophy of meaninglessness was essentially an instrument of liberation from a certain system of morality. We objected to the morality because it interfered with our sexual freedom.'[3]

The argument cuts both ways then. The person who says, 'Your belief in God is just because you have psychological reasons for wanting God to exist' is open to the same charge back, namely, 'Your unbelief is because you have psychological reasons for not wanting God to exist.'

To sum up, as human beings we do have deep psychological needs. The atheist claims Christians have invented God to satisfy these longings. The Christian claims that faith in God meets these needs precisely because God is there and we were made for relationship with him. How do you decide who is right?

The evidence of history

The question must be, 'What is the evidence for God?' That brings us to the heart of the Christian claims. The evidence for God is not that faith works and satisfies our psychological needs. The argument is not, 'Christian faith gives me comfort, hope and peace, so it must be true.' It's the other way round. The argument is, 'Christian faith is true, and that is why it gives me comfort and hope.' In other words the claim is not, 'It works, and that proves it's true,' but rather, 'It's true, and that's why it works.' But how do we know it's true? The answer, in a word, is Jesus.

Christian faith is in the person Jesus Christ. In Jesus, God the Son became a man at a point in history. He was born and lived in first-century Palestine. He did miracles to prove his identity. He died for our sins. He was raised to life. He returned to heaven. These events fulfilled detailed prophecies made in the Old Testament Scriptures hundreds of years before. The New Testament gospel accounts are first-century eye-witness testimonies about him. The evidence is all there. It is simply a fact of history that from the mid-to-first century onwards Christian churches started spreading all over the world, proclaiming Jesus is Lord. Where did these churches come from unless the Jesus events related in the Gospels actually happened? Jesus was not a psychological crutch. He's real – a man of history.

This historical emphasis is central in the New Testament documents. John writes, 'The Word became flesh and made his dwelling among us. We have seen his glory.'[4] Peter writes, 'For we did not follow cleverly devised stories when we told you about the coming of our Lord Jesus Christ in power, but we were eye-witnesses of his majesty.'[5] Luke says he is writing 'an orderly account' based on 'eye-witnesses' having himself 'carefully investigated everything from the beginning.'[6] Paul, speaking to a king about the life of Jesus, says, 'I am convinced that none of this has escaped his notice, because it was not done in a corner.'[7]

It has been said that Christianity is the only falsifiable religion, because it is the only one built on historical events that can be investigated. Other religions are based on someone's private experience, whereas the Christian faith is rooted in public events – the life, death and resurrection of Jesus Christ – which if they happened prove it is true, and if they didn't happen prove it false.

That being the case, the best way forward for someone who is sceptical is to examine the evidence for yourself by reading one of the gospel accounts about Jesus. Take a closer look at him. Countless people have done so over the years, have become convinced, and have become his followers. Are all of them weak, unintelligent, desperate people who felt the need for a crutch to get them through life?

C. S. Lewis described himself on the night he started to follow Christ as 'the most dejected and reluctant convert in all England'.[8] A crutch was the last thing he was looking for. Alistair McGrath, a Professor at Oxford University, says, 'I was … totally convinced there was no God and that anyone who thought there was needed to be locked up for their own good.'[9] It was through his reading and research that he became convinced otherwise. Or take the example of the two Hitchens brothers. Both were highly intelligent and capable men. Both grew up convinced atheists. But Peter then became a Christian, whereas Christopher continued as an atheist until his death from cancer. The 'crutch for the weak' argument simply doesn't fit the range of people who become followers of Jesus and their reasons for doing so.

Deeper needs

When you do take a closer look at Jesus, it becomes clear that our needs are not just psychological. We don't just need hope and meaning and purpose in life – we need forgiveness of sins and rescue from a coming judgement. We need not just feelings in us to change – we need our broken relationship with God to be fixed. On one occasion, recorded in Mark's Gospel, four men carried a paralysed man to Jesus. When Jesus saw their faith he said to the man, 'Your sins are forgiven.'[10] Jesus revealed that the paralysed man's biggest need wasn't actually physical healing but having his sins forgiven so he could be reconciled to God. That is the biggest need we all have.

One day each of us will stand before God, our Creator and Judge. Jesus taught that we will leave that encounter either to enjoy eternal life with him in a world made new, or to suffer eternal alienation from him and his goodness in hell. That is why we need a lot more than a crutch. A crutch is for someone who just needs a bit of help. But as human beings we haven't only a twisted ankle or a broken leg. We're spiritually dead in our sins and under God's judgement. We need life. We need forgiveness. And so we need Jesus.

We need the Jesus who said, 'I am the bread of life … Whoever eats this bread will live for ever'[11]; 'I am the resurrection and the life. The one who believes in me will live, even though they die'[12]; 'I am the light of the world. Whoever follows me will never walk in darkness, but will have the light of life'[13]; 'I am the good shepherd. The good shepherd lays down his life for the sheep'[14]; and, 'I am the way and the truth and the life. No one comes to the Father except through me.'[15]

The delusion is not God or Christian faith. The delusion is the idea that there is no God and we don't need Jesus. God really is there, and Jesus is the only way to him. If this man isn't at least worth a closer look, I don't know what is!

Notes

1. Paralympic Medallist – Stef Reid

1. Romans 3:23.

2. *The Telegraph*, 17 July 2017.

2. Rothschild Rainmaker – Akeel Sachak

1. *The Grocer*, 1 December 2012.

2. *The Telegraph*, 10 December 2006.

3. Premier League Footballer – Gavin Peacock

1. Sid Lowe, *Fear and Loathing in La Liga: Barcelona vs Read Madrid* (Yellow Jersey, 2013).

2. 1 Thessalonians 1:9–10.

3. Philippians 1:21.

4. Oxford Professor – John Lennox

1. *The Wall Street Journal*, 12 October 2007.

2. Richard Dawkins, *The Selfish Gene* (OUP, 1976).

3. Richard Dawkins, *The God Delusion* (Bantam, 2006).

4. John Lennox, *God's Undertaker* (Lion Hudson, 2007).

5. John Lennox, *Gunning for God* (Lion Books, 2011), p. 9.

6. Ibid., p. 15.

7. This, and any other unattributed quotations in this chapter, are from an interview with John Lennox.

8. *Gunning for God*, p. 68.

9. Ibid., p. 73.

10. *God's Undertaker*, p. 21.

11. John Lennox, *God and Stephen Hawking* (Lion Books, 2011), p. 12.

12. *God's Undertaker*, p. 14.

13. *Gunning for God*, p. 56.

14. John Lennox, *Seven Days that Divide the World* (Zondervan, 2011), p. 165.

15. God's Undertaker, p. 61.

16. Ibid., p. 70.

17. Ibid., p. 70.

18. Ibid., p. 71.

19. *God and Stephen Hawking*, p. 56.

20. *God's Undertaker*, p. 67.

21. *God and Stephen Hawking*, p. 29.

22. Stephen Hawking and Leonard Mlodinow, *The Grand Design* (Bantam, 2011).

23. *God and Stephen Hawking*, p. 15.

24. Ibid., p. 37.

25. Ibid., p. 41.

26. Ibid., p. 32.

27. Ibid., p. 95.

28. *God's Undertaker*, p. 122.

29. Ibid., p. 124.

30. Ibid., p. 128.

31. Ibid., p. 129.

32. *Seven Days that Divide the World*, p. 100.

33. *God's Undertaker*, p. 181.

34. Ibid., p. 180.

35. Ibid., p. 163.

36. Ibid., p. 167.

37. Ibid., p. 171.

38. Ibid., p. 208.

39. Ibid., pp. 208–9.

40. Ibid., p. 209.

41. *Gunning for God*, p. 187.

42. *God and Stephen Hawking*, p. 94.

43. *Seven Days that Divide the World*, p. 113.

44. Ibid., p. 114.

45. Ibid., p. 114.

46. *God and Stephen Hawking*, p. 95.

47. *Gunning for God*, p. 15.

5. Bank CEO – Jeremy Marshall

1. Matthew 25:27.

2. 1 Timothy 6:10.

3. Hebrews 13:5.

4. Mark 4:35–41.

7. *Bake Off* Star – Martha Collison

1. Martha Collison, *Twist: Creative Ideas to Reinvent Your Baking* (Harper Collins, 2016).

2. Martha Collison, *Crave: Brilliantly Indulgent Recipes* (Harper Collins, 2017).

3. Luke 14:15 24.

4. Revelation 3:20.

8. Metals Trader – Michael Farmer

1. *The Times*, 28 October 2014.

2. Psalm 119:18 (NASB translation).

3. See Acts 9.

4. Deuteronomy 8:17–18.

5. Matthew 6:3–4.

6. John 3:16.

9. Major General – Tim Cross

1. John 1:29.

2. See Acts 9 and Luke 24:13–35.

10. Cabinet Minister – Jonathan Aitken

1. Jonathan Aitken, *John Newton* (Crossway, 2013), p. 11.

2. Jonathan Aitken, *Pride and Perjury* (Harper Collins, 2000).

3. *Pride and Perjury*, p. 367.

4. Ibid., p. 9.

5. Ibid., p. 366.

6. Jonathan Aitken, *Porridge and Passion* (Continuum International Publishing Group, 2005).

7. Ibid., p. 1.

8. Ibid., pp. 29–30.

9. Jonathan Aiken, *Psalms for People under Pressure* (Bloomsbury, 2004), pp. xii–xiii.

10. Ibid., pp. xvii–xviii.

11. Ibid., p. xv.

12. *Pride and Perjury*, p. 363.

13. Ibid., p. 367.

11. Insurance Executive – Richard Borgonon

1. William Taylor and Richard Borgonon, *The Word One to One* (10Publishing, 2013).

2. John 20:31.

12. Fashion Leader – Simon Ward

1. Simon Ward, *The Character of Fashion* (White Bench, 2016).

2. Simon Ward, *Riding the Tide* (River Publishing & Media, 2013).

13. Opera Singer – Jacques Imbrailo

1. *What's on Stage*, October 2016.

2. The *Financial Times*, May 2010.

3. *The Guardian*, May 2010.

4. All these reviews can be found on intermusica.co.uk (http://bit.ly/2n9gACo)

5. *BBC Music Magazine*, April 2013.

6. *The Times*, 30 April 2010.

7. Ibid.

14. Directors' PA – Yvonne Edwards

1. Luke 7:42–43.

Epilogue

1. Sigmund Freud, *The Future of an Illusion* (Hogarth Press, 1928).

2. Thomas Nagel, *The Last Word* (Oxford University Press, 1997), pp. 130–31.

3. Aldous Huxley, *Ends and Means* (Transaction Publishers, 2012).

4. John 1:14.

5. 2 Peter 1:16.

6. See Luke 1:1–4.

7. Acts 26:26.

8. C.S. Lewis, *Surprised by Joy* (Geoffrey Bles, 1955).

9. Alister McGrath, *The Christian Life and Hope* (SPCK, 2015).

10. Mark 2:5.

11. John 6:48, 51.

12. John 11:25.

13. John 8:12.

14. John 10:11.

15. John 14:6.

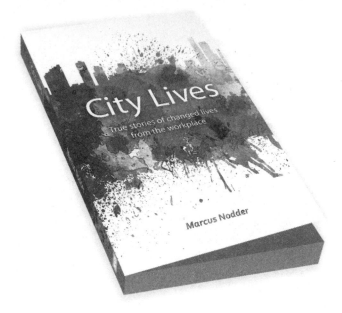

Publishing
a division of 10 of those.com

10Publishing is the publishing house of **10ofThose**. It is committed to producing quality Christian resources that are biblical and accessible.

www.10ofthose.com is our online retail arm selling thousands of quality books at discounted prices.

For information contact: **info@10ofthose.com** or check out our website: **www.10ofthose.com**